# Reading With Ease:
# An Alternative Method

By

## Elaine M. Peters. MSc. Ed.

# Copyright

**Copyright @ 2020 by Elaine M. Peters. MSc. Ed.**
*Reading With Ease: An Alternative Method, Series 1, Volume I*



**ISBN:** 978-1-965007-50-1

# Dedication

To my daughter, whose perseverance and kind heart continue to inspire me.

To my husband and my son, who have provided the unwavering support I required to complete this book.

# About the Author

Elaine Marsha Peters, born 1956 in Toronto, Ontario, Canada, earned an Honors B.A. in Physical Health Education, followed later in life with a Master of Science in Education. Since 1993, Elaine has been a strong advocate and teacher for children, youth, and adults who learn differently. She served as Chair on Parent-Teacher counsels, co-founded a charitable non-profit organization committed to enhancing the lives of adolescents and adults with developmental disabilities through social inclusion, and most recently, has written procedural guides for improving the reading skills of non-readers using research-based alternative methods she developed during her Master of Science in Education practicum.

# Contents

# Synopsis

As a concerned and deeply engaged parent of a child with moderately severe autism and an intellectual disability, discovering there was a vast gap in the quality of education available for our daughter was challenging. The positive aspect of the challenges we faced advocating for education curriculum, instruction, and assessment equality, is this (and future) series of An Alternative Method for beginner readers. Creating an alternative reader series was a labor of love. Coalescing decades of literacy research such as pre-teaching vocabulary sight words combined with the processes of teaching phonetics paired with word symbols, I created a learning strategy that helped our daughter and others improve their reading skills. Not only did she learn to read but she also developed a desire to continue her own lifelong learning journey into the wonders of written language. This first of seven learning-to-read procedural guides opens the door to the discovery of written language for children, youth, and adults who are unique learners.

# Foreword

I am the mother of an adult learner with moderately severe autism and an intellectual (cognitive) disability. The first of a series of beginner readers was a labor of love, reinforced by my love of helping my own child learn to read. My daughter is over the age of twenty-five. She learned to read by coalescing the processes of learning phonics (letter sounds and how those sounds combine to make syllables, words, and sentences) and pre-teaching vocabulary, which was also coupled with the use of word symbols. Combining these learning strategies helped my daughter learn to read.

In addition, our daughter learned to use the internet for information pertaining to things of interest to her. She browses through magazines and newspapers reading captions under photographs, and reads signs posted in the community. Being a visual-kinesthetic-tactile learner meant I had to find meaningful (i.e., meaningful to her) ways to present a large variety of words to her in a way that she found comprehensible. I began the teaching journey with her by increasing her phonetic awareness through books full of photographs or drawings of objects and activities that included color coded phonemes (distinct units of sound created by certain letters and combinations of letters).

In addition, through my own research, I learned to use symbol-writing software combined with creative ways to illustrate and/or play out the meaning of words and phrases. I modeled each word's syllable cadence, often tapping out the cadence with her. Sometimes an illustration or photograph was not adequate to portray a word's or phrase's meaning. In such cases, I used video clips and role play, acting out a word's definition, which turned out to be helpful. A simple example is the word jump. To scaffold the embedding process (i.e., the meaning of the word) in her mind, assisting representational development, I showed her the word's meaning physically by jumping. Then, I would have her act out the word's meaning by encouraging her to jump.

Practice and rehearsal of various words found in the text that she was reading at the time (whether the text was online, from a book, magazine, newspaper, pamphlet, comic book, etc.) were instrumental in developing her current ability to read. A reading facilitator does not always have to be a parent. A relative, a friend, a peer reading coach from school, or even a high school student earning community service hours can make the phonetics-plus-pre-teaching-vocabulary experience fun and memorable for your loved one.

Here are some literacy research nuggets that I discovered which, when applied with patience, persistence, consistency, and playfulness, influenced my daughter's desire to learn to read as well as her ability to read.

In 1948, Edward William Dolch, PhD, published his original Dolch word list in his book Problems in Reading (Johns, J., Edmond, R., & Mavrogenes, N., 1977). Dolch, a major proponent of the 'whole word' method of beginning reading instruction, based his high-frequency word list on his research of children's books. Thus, Dolch determined some words occurred in children's written material most frequently, from pre-kindergarten to third grade, with a separate list of nouns. Dolch believed that children learning his list of 220 'service words' and the 95 high-frequency nouns would result in speeding their development of reading fluency. And, although there are words in the Dolch word list that can be sounded out using phonetic knowledge, many words cannot and, therefore, must be memorized as 'sight words'. Dolch also believed decodable words were best to be mastered for instant recall. As a result, the creation of the Dolch word list is one of the most frequently used English "words list" that are meant to be easily recognized achieving reading fluency, and is applicable in any language (Johns, Edmond, R., & Mavrogenes, N., 1977).

In the 1950s, and updated in the 1980s, Dr. Edward B. Fry expanded on Dolch's sight word lists and research (Bales, K. 2018). Hence, Fry's Instant Words, often referred to as the 'Fry Words', are ranked in order of frequency, representing the most frequently used words in English. In 1996, Dr. Fry expanded and published a book titled Fry 1000 Instant Words.

Consequently, the Fry Sight Words list is a more modern list of words than the Dolch list. Fry's word list captures the most common 1,000 words that appeared in reading materials commonly used in Grades 3-9 during that period. Fry believed learning all 1,000 words in the Fry list would prepare a learner to read about 90% of the words in a typical book, newspaper, or magazine. The Fry words are listed by the frequency with which they occur and are often broken down into groups of 100. Therefore, the first 100 Fry words are the 100 most frequently occurring words in the English language. Note: Social, technological, and education culture, as well as curriculum changes over time may result in unfamiliar words becoming the frequency norm.

Other researchers recommending the approach of pre-teaching words that appear in the text are I.L. Beck and M.G. McKeown. Beck and McKeown wrote in 2002, Bringing Words to Life: Robust Vocabulary Instruction, and in 2008, Creating Robust Vocabulary: Frequently Asked Questions and Extended Examples, that words that appear in the text need to be clarified for increased comprehension (NSW, not). Researchers also suggest that 'sight word instruction' has been highly effective across individuals for people with moderate and severe disabilities (Browder, D. M., & Xin, Y. P., 1998). Furthermore, functional MRI research supports the use of visual pictures associated with text, as both visual memory and visual mental imagery are both facilitated by frontal-parietal regions of the brain. Thus, finding that visual memory and visual mental imagery rely on similar neural network processes (Slotnick, S.D., 2012).

In addition, research evidence also suggests that developing phonics awareness assists children in decoding unfamiliar words (University of Royal Holloway London, 2017). However, without a solid comprehension of word meaning and phrase meaning, a sentence's meaning will not be understood by the individual reading the sentence (Diakidoy, L., 1998). Furthermore, research evidence supports the use of phonics where a facilitator models the splitting of words into their consonant and vowel sounds, followed by blending those sounds as scaffolded support to learners (Williams, 1980).

Therefore, I have used two colors to assist reading facilitators model the splitting of words into consonant and vowel sounds: consonant sounds are underlined in blue, and vowel sounds are underlined in green. Followed by the thoughtful blending of those sounds to a learner and encouraging the learner to repeat the process back to the reading facilitator, a learner's phonemic awareness and self-confidence will increase with practice.

The twenty short stories within the reading guide combine Dolch and Fry word lists without conforming to their strict frequency word order. Rather, the short stories herein are intended to be entertaining and engaging within a multi-sensory learning experience (that is, visual, auditory, tactile, and kinesthetic) that is driven by the reading facilitator's knowledge and understanding of the individual learner as well as the facilitator's creativity, flexibility, and responsiveness to the learner.

The reading facilitator assists the learner in creating within their mind the meaning of each word, phrase, and sentence.

Lastly, included at the end of each story are word list data sheets for reading facilitators interested in tracking learning success over time. There is also a Master Word List data sheet in the Appendix of this reading guide. This is the first of a series of beginner Reading With Ease: An Alternative Method. I hope your learner is as engaged in the process of learning to read just as my own daughter has been and continues to be.

# References


- Bales, Kris (August 19, 2018). What are Fry Words, Sourced on October 10, 2018. Retrieved from https://www.thoughtco.com/what-are-fry-words-4172175

- Browder D. M & Xin Y. P (1998). A Meta-Analysis and Review of Sight Word Research and Its Implications for Teaching Functional Reading to Individuals with Moderate and Severe Disabilities The Journal of Special Education, 32(3) 130-153. https://doi.org/10.1177/002246699803200301

- Diakidoy, I (1998). The Role of Reading Comprehension in Word Meaning Acquisition During Reading. European Journal of Psychology of Education, 13(2) 131-154. Retrieved from https://www.jstor.org/stable/23420172

- Johns, J., Edmond, R., & Mavrogenes, N. (1977). The Dolch Basic Sight Vocabulary: A Replication and Validation Study. The Elementary School Journal, 78(1) 31-37. https://www.jstor.org/stable/10011155

- NSW Government (n.d.). Vocabulary — Pre-Teaching. NSW Centre for Effective Reading. Sourced on October 10, 2018. Retrieved from https://www.cer.education.nsw.gov.au/documents/249903/250184/Pre-teach%20vocab.pdf

- Slotnick S.D., Thompson W., & Kosslyn S.M. (2012). Visual Memory and Visual Mental Imagery Recruit Common Control and Sensory Regions of the Brain. Cognitive Neuroscience 3:1, 14-20. DOI: 10.1080/17588928.2011.578210

- UEN Utah Education Network (2003). Phrases and Fry Instant Words. Sourced on October 10, 2018 from https://www.uen.org/k2-educator/word_lists.shtml

- University of Royal Holloway London. (2017, April 20). Phonics works: Sounding out words is best way to teach reading, study suggests. ScienceDaily. Retrieved June 20, 2019. Retrieved from www.sciencedaily.com/releases/2017/04/170420094107.htm

- Williams, J P. (1980). Teaching decoding with an emphasis on phoneme analysis and phoneme blending. Journal of Educational Psychology, 72(1) 1-15. https://dx.doi.org/10.1037/0022-0663.72.1.1

# Pre-Teaching Vocabulary

- Review with the learner the first page of illustrated words presented before each story. If possible, print the page of illustrated words for each story.

- Cut out and (if possible) laminate each illustrated word block making sure there are smooth round corners, no sharp corners for safety reasons, on the word blocks. Another option is to print each page of illustrated words onto large label sheets (8.5" x 11"). Then, lay the label sheet of word symbol blocks onto a cardboard sheet (8.5" x 11"), which can be cut from an empty cereal box. Next, cut out each word symbol block making sure to round out the corners, again for safety reasons.

- Have the learner choose a word block.

- The facilitator says the word aloud, slowly, three times, using a pencil or crayon to point to consonant/vowel of a word while making the sound of that consonant/vowel (phonemes). Then, blend the consonant/vowel sounds (phonemes) to say the word.

- The facilitator says to the learner, "Your turn."

- The facilitator assists with pronunciation as needed. Tapping out the cadence of the word's letter sounds is also helpful.

- Act out or role-play to express an action word's meaning. Be creative. Try various ways to elicit positive engagement from the learner. Try using a favorite object/video clip of the learner to act out and make clear a word's meaning.

- Repeat steps 3 to 7 for all ten words. **IMPORTANT**: Provide the learner with a meaningful reward paired with verbal (or signing) "great reading" acknowledgment each time the learner reads a word block accurately. Examples of rewards: verbal or gestural praise such as high fives, smiles, nods, and thumbs ups, or concrete rewards such as favorite stickers, a certain number of minutes playing a video game or watching a video, extra computer time, listening to a favorite riff or song.

- Lay out 3-word blocks at one time face down. The learner selects one at random, saying the word aloud with help from the facilitator, as necessary. (Modification: If the learner is non-verbal, leave the 3-word blocks face up, the facilitator says a word aloud and the learner points to the word block that represents the word spoken by the facilitator. If correctly identified, turn the word block face down. Continue this process until all the word blocks are face down.)

- Lay out the next 3-word blocks face down. Follow step 9 instructions.

- Lay out the remaining 4-word blocks face down. Follow step 9 instructions.

- Lay out all the 10-word blocks face down. The learner selects one at random, saying the word aloud with help from the facilitator, as necessary. (Modification: If the learner is non-verbal. leave the 10-word blocks face up, the facilitator says a word aloud and the learner points to the word block that represents the word spoken by the facilitator. If correctly identified, turn the word block face down. Continue this process until all the word blocks are face down.)

**Consistently delivering the positive reinforcement every time the behavior (reading a word block) occurs is IMPORTANT!**

# Story 1

the
dog
is
sleeping
boy
girl
mother
father
good
night

# Tips for the Reading Facilitator:

Using a sheet of paper, cover all lines/sentences below the line/sentence the learner will read. Once the learner has read the line/sentence (with assistance or independently), uncover the next line/sentence. This technique offers less distraction and more focused attention on the line/sentence to be read.

After the learner reads each line/sentence (with or without assistance), provide positive reinforcement that is meaningful to the learner.
Be creative, use objects or video clips to help exemplify the words being learned.

Use the *Word List Data Sheet* that follows this story to track a learner's progress.

Use the *Master Word List Data Sheet* in the Appendix to track word recognition mastery.

**Note:** Words appearing in previous stories are regarded as being familiar to the learner. However, some review may be necessary to maintain word recognition and understanding.

The story with word symbols begins on the next page.

The dog is sleeping.

The boy is sleeping.

The girl is sleeping.

The mother is sleeping.

The father is sleeping.

Good night.

# Tips for the Reading Facilitator:

Once the learner can fluently read the story with word symbols, have them read the same story shown on the next page which eliminates individual word symbols.

Using a sheet of paper, cover all lines/sentences below the line/sentence the learner will read. Once the learner has read the line/sentence (with assistance or independently), uncover the next line/sentence. This technique offers less distraction and more focused attention on the line/sentence to be read.

After the learner reads each line/sentence (with or without assistance), provide positive reinforcement that is meaningful to the learner.

Be creative, use objects or video clips to help exemplify the words being learned.

Use the *Word List Data Sheet* that follows this story to track a learner's progress.

Use the *Master Word List Data Sheet* in the Appendix to track word recognition mastery.

**Note:** Words appearing in previous stories are regarded as being familiar to the learner. However, some review may be necessary to maintain word recognition and understanding.

The dog is sleeping.

The boy is sleeping.

The girl is sleeping.

The mother is sleeping.

The father is sleeping.

Good night!

# Word List Data Sheets

**(Copy this sheet as often as necessary to track progress over time)**

| Date: | Some Assistance | No Assistance | Date: | Some Assistance | No Assistance | Date: | Some Assistance | No Assistance | Date: | Some Assistance | No Assistance |
|---|---|---|---|---|---|---|---|---|---|---|---|
|  |  |  |  |  |  |  |  |  |  |  |  |
|  |  |  |  |  |  |  |  |  |  |  |  |
|  |  |  |  |  |  |  |  |  |  |  |  |
|  |  |  |  |  |  |  |  |  |  |  |  |
|  |  |  |  |  |  |  |  |  |  |  |  |
|  |  |  |  |  |  |  |  |  |  |  |  |
|  |  |  |  |  |  |  |  |  |  |  |  |
|  |  |  |  |  |  |  |  |  |  |  |  |
|  |  |  |  |  |  |  |  |  |  |  |  |

# Story 2

into
house
ran
a
mouse
cat
sat
in
so
from

# Tips for the Reading Facilitator:

Using a sheet of paper, cover all lines/sentences below the line/sentence the learner will read. Once the learner has read the line/sentence (with assistance or independently), uncover the next line/sentence. This technique offers less distraction and more focused attention on the line/sentence to be read.

After the learner reads each line/sentence (with or without assistance), provide positive reinforcement that is meaningful to the learner.
Be creative, use objects or video clips to help exemplify the words being learned.

Use the *Word List Data Sheet* that follows this story to track a learner's progress.

Use the *Master Word List Data Sheet* in the Appendix to track word recognition mastery.

**Note:** Words appearing in previous stories are regarded as being familiar to the learner. However, some review may be necessary to maintain word recognition and understanding.

The story with word symbols begins on the next page.

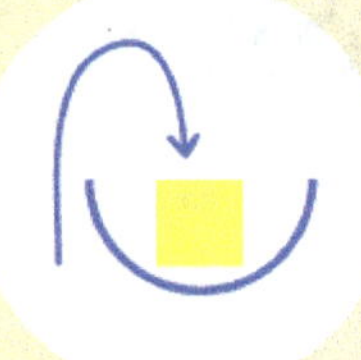 Into the  house  ran  a  mouse.

 A  cat  sat  in  the house.

 So, the  mouse  ran 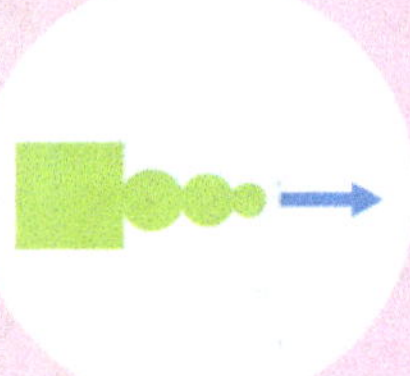 from

 the house.

# Tips for the Reading Facilitator:

Once the learner can fluently read the story with word symbols, have them read the same story shown on the next page which eliminates individual word symbols.

Using a sheet of paper, cover all lines/sentences below the line/sentence the learner will read. Once the learner has read the line/sentence (with assistance or independently), uncover the next line/sentence. This technique offers less distraction and more focused attention on the line/sentence to be read.

After the learner reads each line/sentence (with or without assistance), provide positive reinforcement that is meaningful to the learner.

Be creative, use objects or video clips to help exemplify the words being learned.

Use the *Word List Data Sheet* that follows this story to track a learner's progress.

Use the *Master Word List Data Sheet* in the Appendix to track word recognition mastery.

**Note:** Words appearing in previous stories are regarded as being familiar to the learner. However, some review may be necessary to maintain word recognition and understanding.

Into the house

ran a mouse.

A cat sat in

the house.

So, the mouse

ran from the

house.

# Word List Data Sheets

**(Copy this sheet as often as necessary to track progress over time)**

| Date: | | | Date: | | | Date: | | | Date: | | |
|---|---|---|---|---|---|---|---|---|---|---|---|
| | Some Assistance | No Assistance | Assistance | Some Assistance | No Assistance | Assistance | Some Assistance | No Assistance | Assistance | Some Assistance | No Assistance |
| | | | | | | | | | | | |
| | | | | | | | | | | | |
| | | | | | | | | | | | |
| | | | | | | | | | | | |
| | | | | | | | | | | | |
| | | | | | | | | | | | |
| | | | | | | | | | | | |
| | | | | | | | | | | | |
| | | | | | | | | | | | |
| | | | | | | | | | | | |

**Reading With Ease: An Alternative Method, Series 1, Volume 1**

# Story 3

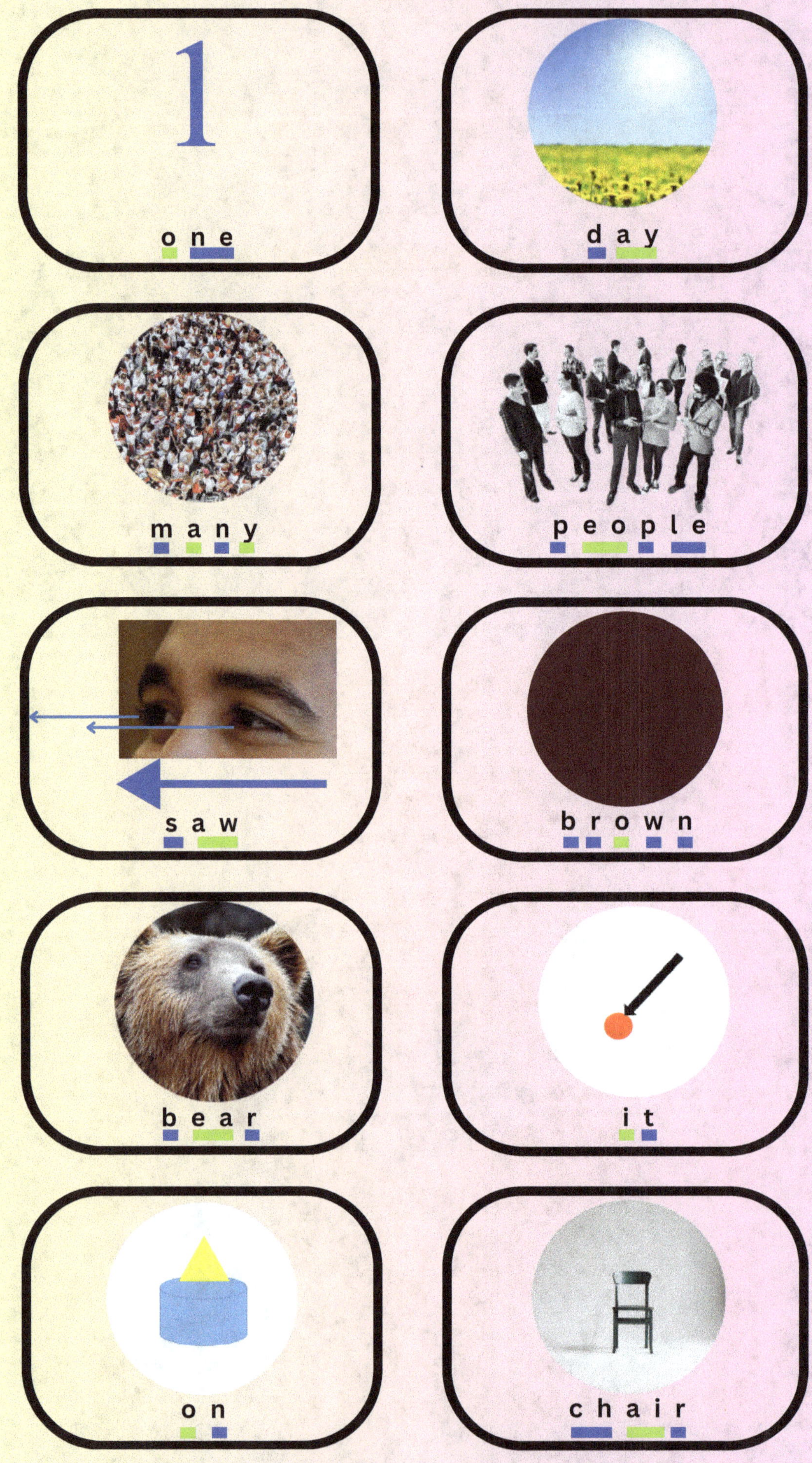


one
day
many
people
saw
brown
bear
it
on
chair

# Tips for the Reading Facilitator:

Using a sheet of paper, cover all lines/sentences below the line/sentence the learner will read. Once the learner has read the line/sentence (with assistance or independently), uncover the next line/sentence. This technique offers less distraction and more focused attention on the line/sentence to be read.

After the learner reads each line/sentence (with or without assistance), provide positive reinforcement that is meaningful to the learner.
Be creative, use objects or video clips to help exemplify the words being learned.

Use the *Word List Data Sheet* that follows this story to track a learner's progress.

Use the *Master Word List Data Sheet* in the Appendix to track word recognition mastery.

**Note:** Words appearing in previous stories are regarded as being familiar to the learner. However, some review may be necessary to maintain word recognition and understanding.

The story with word symbols begins on the next page.

**1** One day many people

saw a brown bear.

It sat on a chair.

# Tips for the Reading Facilitator:

Once the learner can fluently read the story with word symbols, have them read the same story shown on the next page which eliminates individual word symbols.

Using a sheet of paper, cover all lines/sentences below the line/sentence the learner will read. Once the learner has read the line/sentence (with assistance or independently), uncover the next line/sentence. This technique offers less distraction and more focused attention on the line/sentence to be read.

After the learner reads each line/sentence (with or without assistance), provide positive reinforcement that is meaningful to the learner.

Be creative, use objects or video clips to help exemplify the words being learned.

Use the *Word List Data Sheet* that follows this story to track a learner's progress.

Use the *Master Word List Data Sheet* in the Appendix to track word recognition mastery.

**Note:** Words appearing in previous stories are regarded as being familiar to the learner. However, some review may be necessary to maintain word recognition and understanding.

Elaine M. Peters

One day many
people

saw a brown
bear.

It sat on a
chair.

# Word List Data Sheets

**(Copy this sheet as often as necessary to track progress over time)**

| Date: | | | Date: | | | Date: | | | Date: | | |
|---|---|---|---|---|---|---|---|---|---|---|---|
| Assistance | Some Assistance | No Assistance | Assistance | Some Assistance | No Assistance | Assistance | Some Assistance | No Assistance | Assistance | Some Assistance | No Assistance |
| | | | | | | | | | | | |
| | | | | | | | | | | | |
| | | | | | | | | | | | |
| | | | | | | | | | | | |
| | | | | | | | | | | | |
| | | | | | | | | | | | |
| | | | | | | | | | | | |
| | | | | | | | | | | | |
| | | | | | | | | | | | |
| | | | | | | | | | | | |

**Reading With Ease: An Alternative Method, Series 1, Volume 1**

# Story 4

an
elephant
can
you
squirt
water
its
trunk
your
nose

# Tips for the Reading Facilitator:

Using a sheet of paper, cover all lines/sentences below the line/sentence the learner will read. Once the learner has read the line/sentence (with assistance or independently), uncover the next line/sentence. This technique offers less distraction and more focused attention on the line/sentence to be read.

After the learner reads each line/sentence (with or without assistance), provide positive reinforcement that is meaningful to the learner.
Be creative, use objects or video clips to help exemplify the words being learned.

Use the *Word List Data Sheet* that follows this story to track a learner's progress.

Use the *Master Word List Data Sheet* in the Appendix to track word recognition mastery.

**Note:** Words appearing in previous stories are regarded as being familiar to the learner. However, some review may be necessary to maintain word recognition and understanding.

The story with word symbols begins on the next page.

An     elephant     can     squirt

water     from     its     trunk.

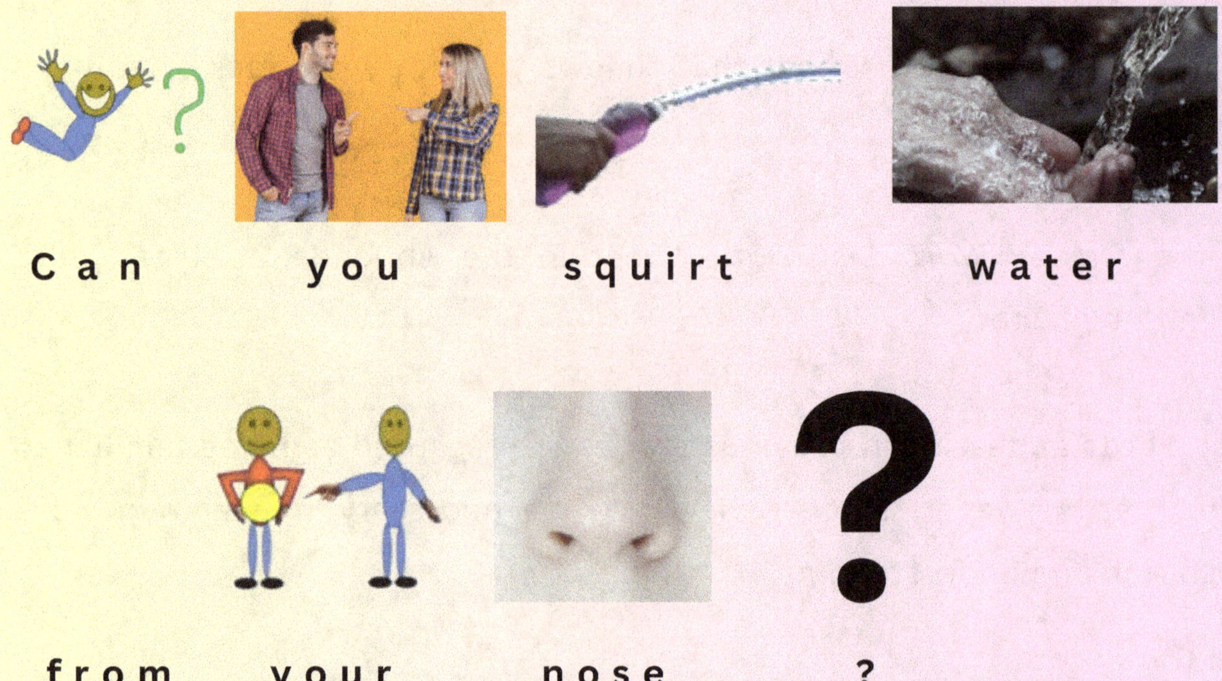

Can     you     squirt     water

from     your     nose     ?

# Tips for the Reading Facilitator:

Once the learner can fluently read the story with word symbols, have them read the same story shown on the next page which eliminates individual word symbols.

Using a sheet of paper, cover all lines/sentences below the line/sentence the learner will read. Once the learner has read the line/sentence (with assistance or independently), uncover the next line/sentence. This technique offers less distraction and more focused attention on the line/sentence to be read.

After the learner reads each line/sentence (with or without assistance), provide positive reinforcement that is meaningful to the learner.

Be creative, use objects or video clips to help exemplify the words being learned.

Use the *Word List Data Sheet* that follows this story to track a learner's progress.

Use the *Master Word List Data Sheet* in the Appendix to track word recognition mastery.

**Note:** Words appearing in previous stories are regarded as being familiar to the learner. However, some review may be necessary to maintain word recognition and understanding.

An elephant
can squirt
water from
its trunk.

Can you
squirt water
from your
nose?

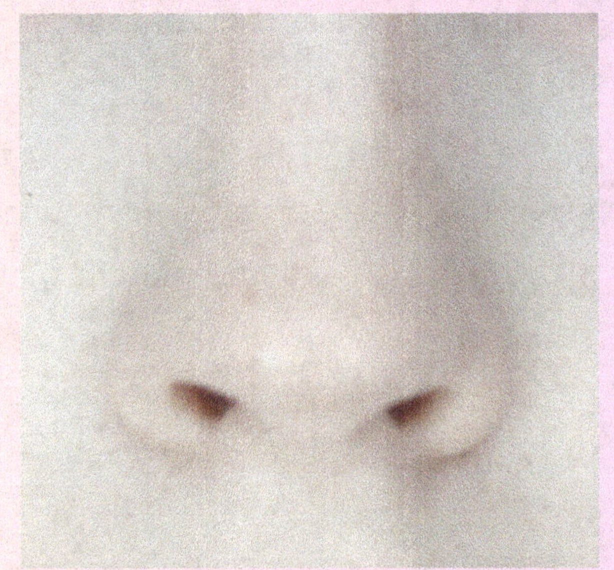

# Word List Data Sheets

**(Copy this sheet as often as necessary to track progress over time)**

| Date: | | | Date: | | | Date: | | | Date: | | |
|---|---|---|---|---|---|---|---|---|---|---|---|
| Assistance | Some Assistance | No Assistance | Assistance | Some Assistance | No Assistance | Assistance | Some Assistance | No Assistance | Assistance | Some Assistance | No Assistance |
| | | | | | | | | | | | |
| | | | | | | | | | | | |
| | | | | | | | | | | | |
| | | | | | | | | | | | |
| | | | | | | | | | | | |
| | | | | | | | | | | | |
| | | | | | | | | | | | |
| | | | | | | | | | | | |
| | | | | | | | | | | | |
| | | | | | | | | | | | |

**Reading With Ease: An Alternative Method, Series 1, Volume 1**

# Story 5

and
sit
under
tree
see
sea
write
they
stories
about

# Tips for the Reading Facilitator:

Using a sheet of paper, cover all lines/sentences below the line/sentence the learner will read. Once the learner has read the line/sentence (with assistance or independently), uncover the next line/sentence. This technique offers less distraction and more focused attention on the line/sentence to be read.

After the learner reads each line/sentence (with or without assistance), provide positive reinforcement that is meaningful to the learner.
Be creative, use objects or video clips to help exemplify the words being learned.

Use the *Word List Data Sheet* that follows this story to track a learner's progress.

Use the *Master Word List Data Sheet* in the Appendix to track word recognition mastery.

**Note:** Words appearing in previous stories are regarded as being familiar to the learner. However, some review may be necessary to maintain word recognition and understanding.

The story with word symbols begins on the next page.

 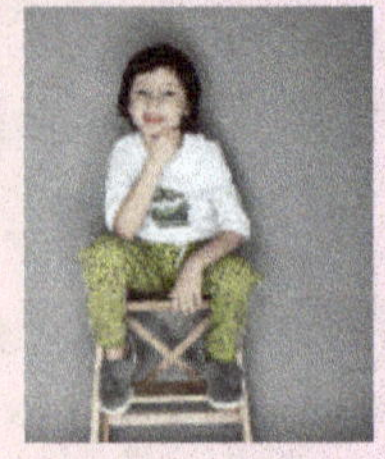 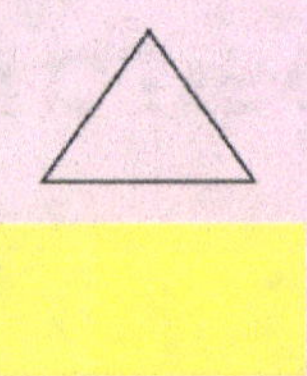

&+

A    boy   and   a   girl   sit   under

a    tree.

 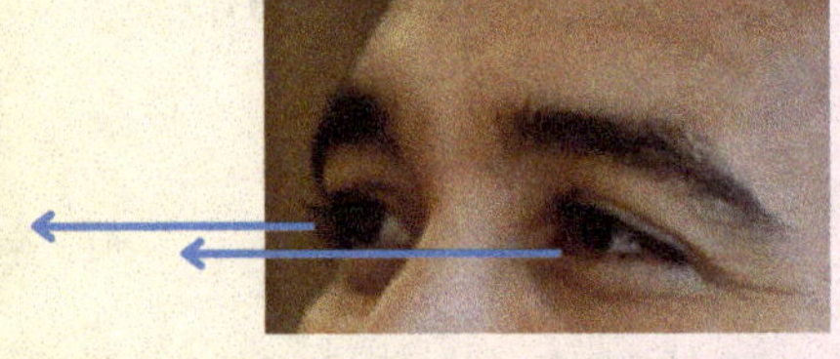 

They   see   the   sea

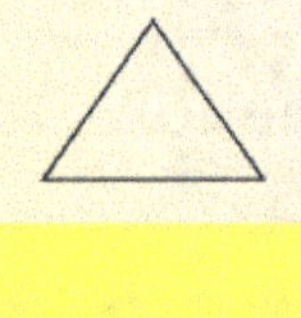 

from   under   the   tree.

  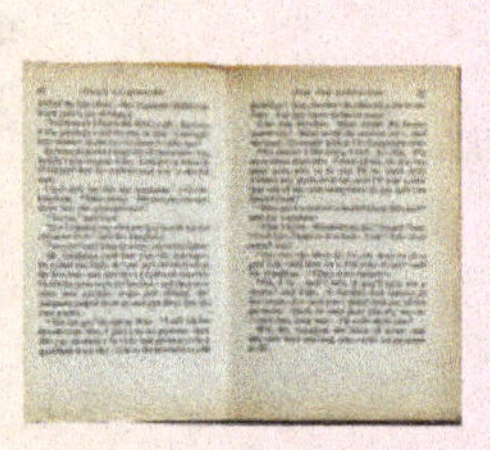 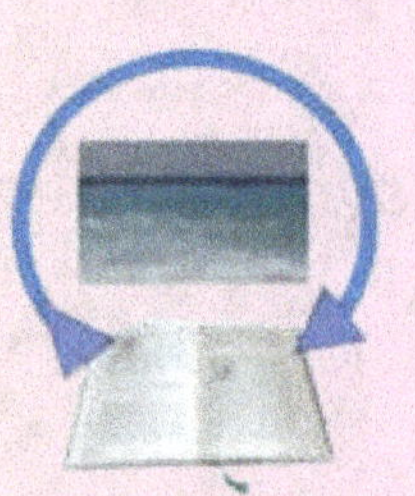 

They   write   stories   about   the   sea.

# Tips for the Reading Facilitator:

Once the learner can fluently read the story with word symbols, have them read the same story shown on the next page which eliminates individual word symbols.

Using a sheet of paper, cover all lines/sentences below the line/sentence the learner will read. Once the learner has read the line/sentence (with assistance or independently), uncover the next line/sentence. This technique offers less distraction and more focused attention on the line/sentence to be read.

After the learner reads each line/sentence (with or without assistance), provide positive reinforcement that is meaningful to the learner.

Be creative, use objects or video clips to help exemplify the words being learned.

Use the *Word List Data Sheet* that follows this story to track a learner's progress.

Use the *Master Word List Data Sheet* in the Appendix to track word recognition mastery.

**Note:** Words appearing in previous stories are regarded as being familiar to the learner. However, some review may be necessary to maintain word recognition and understanding.

A boy and a girl sit under a tree.

They see the sea from under the tree.

They write stories about the sea.

# Word List Data Sheets

**(Copy this sheet as often as necessary to track progress over time)**

| Date: | | | Date: | | | Date: | | | Date: | | |
|---|---|---|---|---|---|---|---|---|---|---|---|
| Assistance | Some Assistance | No Assistance | Assistance | Some Assistance | No Assistance | Assistance | Some Assistance | No Assistance | Assistance | Some Assistance | No Assistance |
| | | | | | | | | | | | |
| | | | | | | | | | | | |
| | | | | | | | | | | | |
| | | | | | | | | | | | |
| | | | | | | | | | | | |
| | | | | | | | | | | | |
| | | | | | | | | | | | |
| | | | | | | | | | | | |
| | | | | | | | | | | | |
| | | | | | | | | | | | |

**Reading With Ease: An Alternative Method, Series 1, Volume 1**

# Story 6

we
watch
their
two
dogs
play
all
laugh
for
fun

# Tips for the Reading Facilitator:

Using a sheet of paper, cover all lines/sentences below the line/sentence the learner will read. Once the learner has read the line/sentence (with assistance or independently), uncover the next line/sentence. This technique offers less distraction and more focused attention on the line/sentence to be read.

After the learner reads each line/sentence (with or without assistance), provide positive reinforcement that is meaningful to the learner.
Be creative, use objects or video clips to help exemplify the words being learned.

Use the *Word List Data Sheet* that follows this story to track a learner's progress.

Use the *Master Word List Data Sheet* in the Appendix to track word recognition mastery.

**Note:** Words appearing in previous stories are regarded as being familiar to the learner. However, some review may be necessary to maintain word recognition and understanding.

The story with word symbols begins on the next page.

 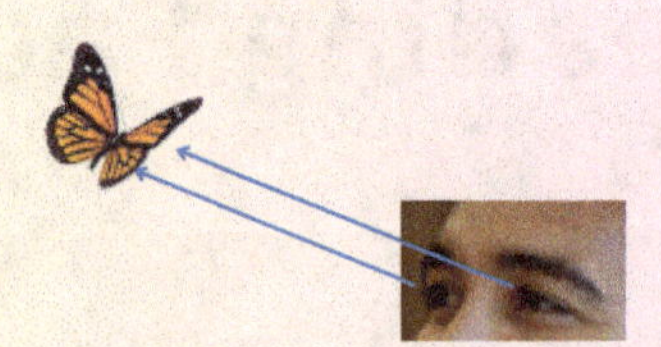 

We can watch their two

dogs play all day.

We laugh.

The dogs play for fun !

# Tips for the Reading Facilitator:

Once the learner can fluently read the story with word symbols, have them read the same story shown on the next page which eliminates individual word symbols.

Using a sheet of paper, cover all lines/sentences below the line/sentence the learner will read. Once the learner has read the line/sentence (with assistance or independently), uncover the next line/sentence. This technique offers less distraction and more focused attention on the line/sentence to be read.

After the learner reads each line/sentence (with or without assistance), provide positive reinforcement that is meaningful to the learner.

Be creative, use objects or video clips to help exemplify the words being learned.

Use the *Word List Data Sheet* that follows this story to track a learner's progress.

Use the *Master Word List Data Sheet* in the Appendix to track word recognition mastery.

**Note:** Words appearing in previous stories are regarded as being familiar to the learner. However, some review may be necessary to maintain word recognition and understanding.

We can watch their two
dogs play all day.

We laugh.

The dogs play for fun!

# Word List Data Sheets

**(Copy this sheet as often as necessary to track progress over time)**

| Date: | | | Date: | | | Date: | | | Date: | | |
|---|---|---|---|---|---|---|---|---|---|---|---|
| Assistance | Some Assistance | No Assistance | Assistance | Some Assistance | No Assistance | Assistance | Some Assistance | No Assistance | Assistance | Some Assistance | No Assistance |
| | | | | | | | | | | | |
| | | | | | | | | | | | |
| | | | | | | | | | | | |
| | | | | | | | | | | | |
| | | | | | | | | | | | |
| | | | | | | | | | | | |
| | | | | | | | | | | | |
| | | | | | | | | | | | |
| | | | | | | | | | | | |
| | | | | | | | | | | | |

**Reading With Ease: An Alternative Method, Series 1, Volume 1**

# Story 7

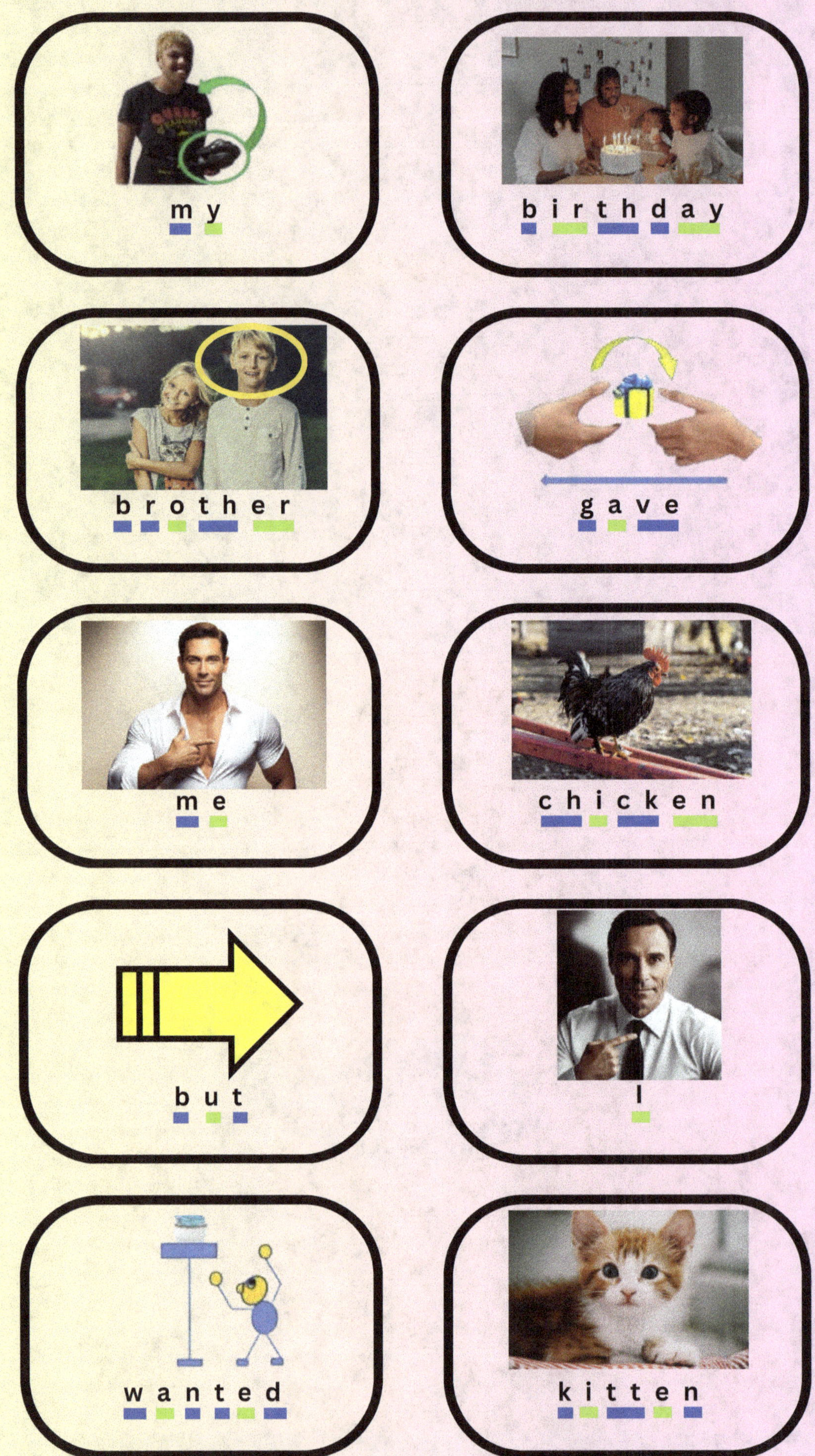


my
birthday
brother
gave
me
chicken
but
I
wanted
kitten

# Tips for the Reading Facilitator:

Using a sheet of paper, cover all lines/sentences below the line/sentence the learner will read. Once the learner has read the line/sentence (with assistance or independently), uncover the next line/sentence. This technique offers less distraction and more focused attention on the line/sentence to be read.

After the learner reads each line/sentence (with or without assistance), provide positive reinforcement that is meaningful to the learner.
Be creative, use objects or video clips to help exemplify the words being learned.

Use the *Word List Data Sheet* that follows this story to track a learner's progress.

Use the *Master Word List Data Sheet* in the Appendix to track word recognition mastery.

**Note:** Words appearing in previous stories are regarded as being familiar to the learner. However, some review may be necessary to maintain word recognition and understanding.

The story with word symbols begins on the next page.

**For my birthday, my brother**

**gave me a chicken.**

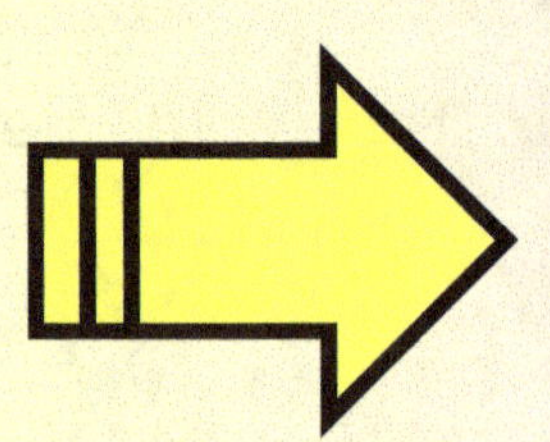   

**But I wanted a kitten.**

# Tips for the Reading Facilitator:

Once the learner can fluently read the story with word symbols, have them read the same story shown on the next page which eliminates individual word symbols.

Using a sheet of paper, cover all lines/sentences below the line/sentence the learner will read. Once the learner has read the line/sentence (with assistance or independently), uncover the next line/sentence. This technique offers less distraction and more focused attention on the line/sentence to be read.

After the learner reads each line/sentence (with or without assistance), provide positive reinforcement that is meaningful to the learner.

Be creative, use objects or video clips to help exemplify the words being learned.

Use the *Word List Data Sheet* that follows this story to track a learner's progress.

Use the *Master Word List Data Sheet* in the Appendix to track word recognition mastery.

**Note:** Words appearing in previous stories are regarded as being familiar to the learner. However, some review may be necessary to maintain word recognition and understanding.

For my birthday, my brother gave me a chicken.

But I wanted a kitten.

# Word List Data Sheets

**(Copy this sheet as often as necessary to track progress over time)**

| Date: | Some Assistance | No Assistance | Date: | Some Assistance | No Assistance | Date: | Some Assistance | No Assistance | Date: | Some Assistance | No Assistance |
|---|---|---|---|---|---|---|---|---|---|---|---|
| Assistance | | | Assistance | | | Assistance | | | Assistance | | |
| | | | | | | | | | | | |
| | | | | | | | | | | | |
| | | | | | | | | | | | |
| | | | | | | | | | | | |
| | | | | | | | | | | | |
| | | | | | | | | | | | |
| | | | | | | | | | | | |
| | | | | | | | | | | | |
| | | | | | | | | | | | |
| | | | | | | | | | | | |

**Reading With Ease: An Alternative Method, Series 1, Volume 1**

# Story 8

some
make
games
trains
planes
do
know
person
who
makes

# Tips for the Reading Facilitator:

Using a sheet of paper, cover all lines/sentences below the line/sentence the learner will read. Once the learner has read the line/sentence (with assistance or independently), uncover the next line/sentence. This technique offers less distraction and more focused attention on the line/sentence to be read.

After the learner reads each line/sentence (with or without assistance), provide positive reinforcement that is meaningful to the learner.
Be creative, use objects or video clips to help exemplify the words being learned.

Use the *Word List Data Sheet* that follows this story to track a learner's progress.

Use the *Master Word List Data Sheet* in the Appendix to track word recognition mastery.

**Note:** Words appearing in previous stories are regarded as being familiar to the learner. However, some review may be necessary to maintain word recognition and understanding.

The story with word symbols begins on the next page.

Some people make games.

Some people make trains.

Do you know a person

who makes planes ?

# Tips for the Reading Facilitator:

Once the learner can fluently read the story with word symbols, have them read the same story shown on the next page which eliminates individual word symbols.

Using a sheet of paper, cover all lines/sentences below the line/sentence the learner will read. Once the learner has read the line/sentence (with assistance or independently), uncover the next line/sentence. This technique offers less distraction and more focused attention on the line/sentence to be read.

After the learner reads each line/sentence (with or without assistance), provide positive reinforcement that is meaningful to the learner.

Be creative, use objects or video clips to help exemplify the words being learned.

Use the *Word List Data Sheet* that follows this story to track a learner's progress.

Use the *Master Word List Data Sheet* in the Appendix to track word recognition mastery.

**Note:** Words appearing in previous stories are regarded as being familiar to the learner. However, some review may be necessary to maintain word recognition and understanding.

# Some people make games.

# Some people make trains.

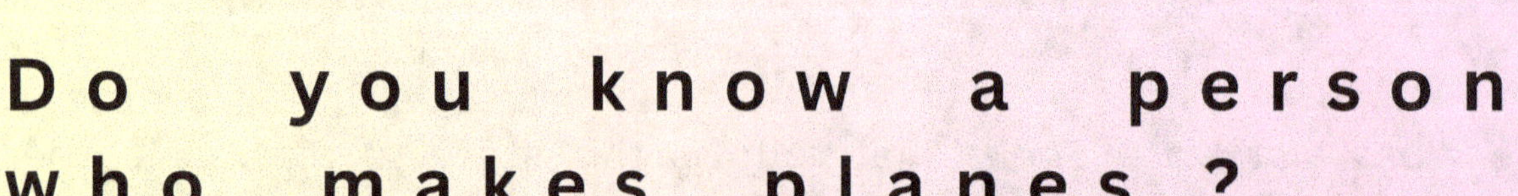

# Do you know a person who makes planes?

# Word List Data Sheets

**(Copy this sheet as often as necessary to track progress over time)**

| Date: | | | Date: | | | Date: | | | Date: | | |
|---|---|---|---|---|---|---|---|---|---|---|---|
| ...stance | Some Assistance | No Assistance | Assistance | Some Assistance | No Assistance | Assistance | Some Assistance | No Assistance | Assistance | Some Assistance | No Assistance |
| | | | | | | | | | | | |
| | | | | | | | | | | | |
| | | | | | | | | | | | |
| | | | | | | | | | | | |
| | | | | | | | | | | | |
| | | | | | | | | | | | |
| | | | | | | | | | | | |
| | | | | | | | | | | | |
| | | | | | | | | | | | |
| | | | | | | | | | | | |

**Reading With Ease: An Alternative Method, Series 1, Volume 1**

# Story 9

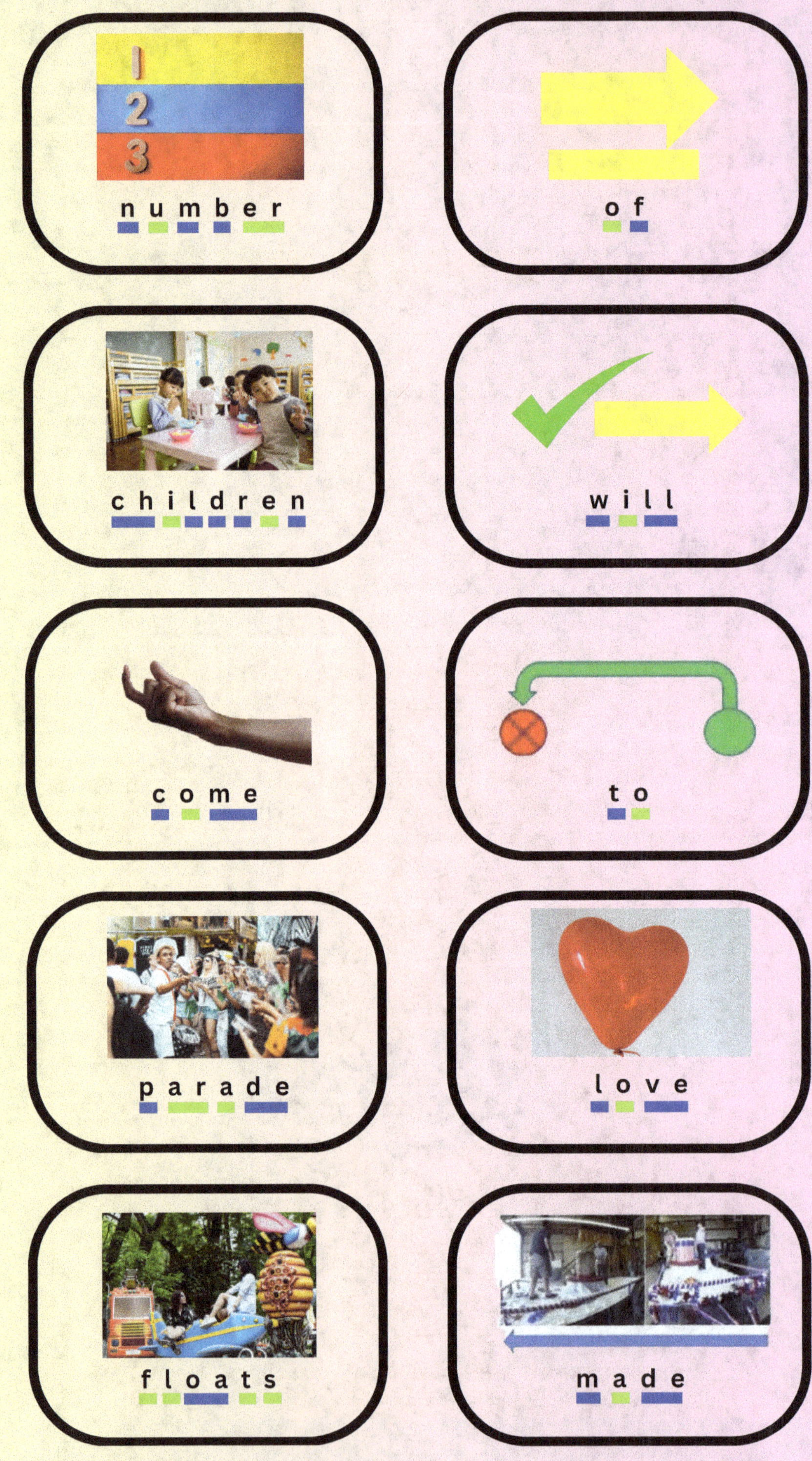

number
of
children
will
come
to
parade
love
floats
made

# Tips for the Reading Facilitator:

Using a sheet of paper, cover all lines/sentences below the line/sentence the learner will read. Once the learner has read the line/sentence (with assistance or independently), uncover the next line/sentence. This technique offers less distraction and more focused attention on the line/sentence to be read.

After the learner reads each line/sentence (with or without assistance), provide positive reinforcement that is meaningful to the learner.
Be creative, use objects or video clips to help exemplify the words being learned.

Use the *Word List Data Sheet* that follows this story to track a learner's progress.

Use the *Master Word List Data Sheet* in the Appendix to track word recognition mastery.

**Note:** Words appearing in previous stories are regarded as being familiar to the learner. However, some review may be necessary to maintain word recognition and understanding.

The story with word symbols begins on the next page.

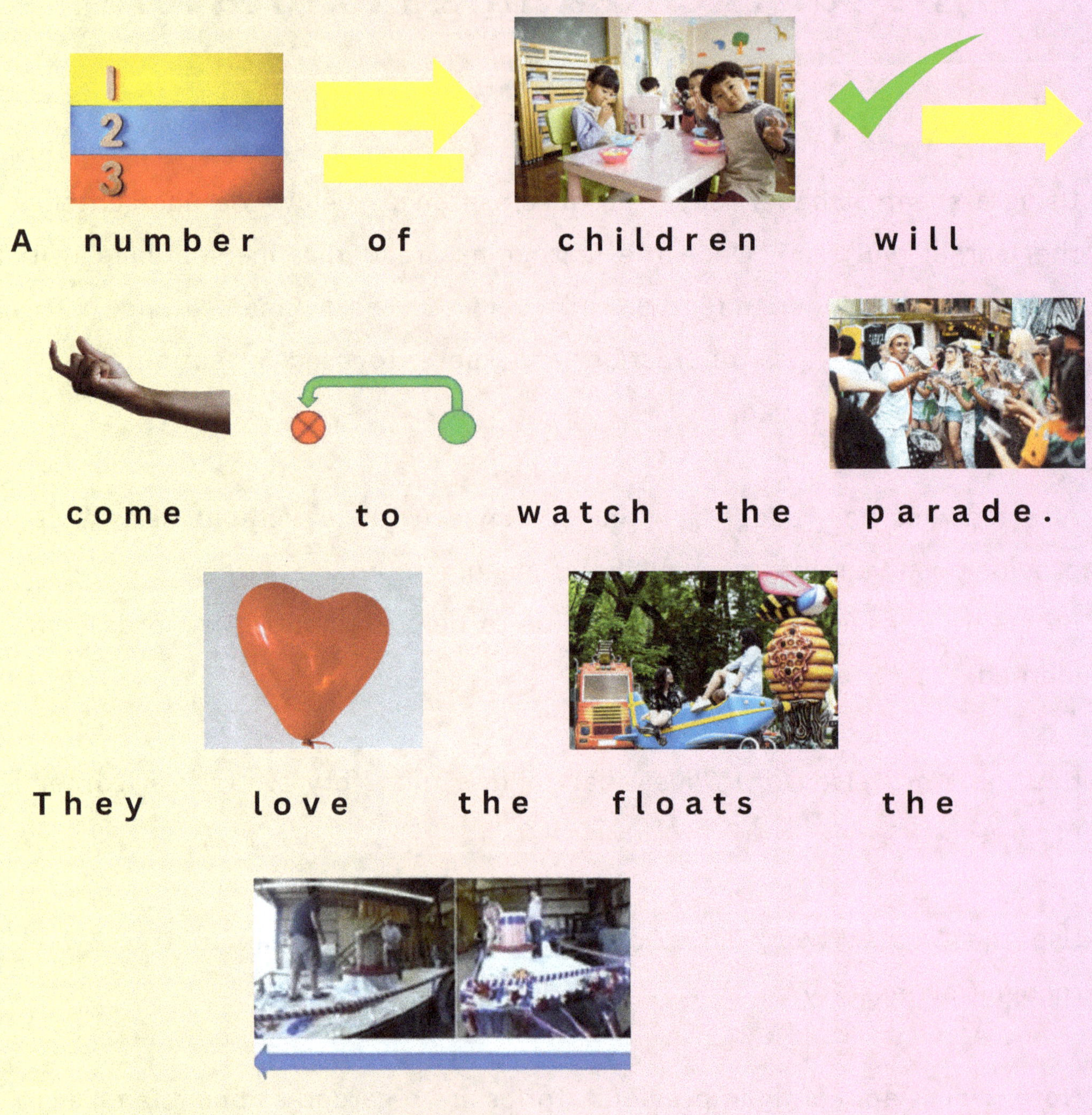

A number of children will come to watch the parade. They love the floats the people made.

# Tips for the Reading Facilitator:

Once the learner can fluently read the story with word symbols, have them read the same story shown on the next page which eliminates individual word symbols.

Using a sheet of paper, cover all lines/sentences below the line/sentence the learner will read. Once the learner has read the line/sentence (with assistance or independently), uncover the next line/sentence. This technique offers less distraction and more focused attention on the line/sentence to be read.

After the learner reads each line/sentence (with or without assistance), provide positive reinforcement that is meaningful to the learner.

Be creative, use objects or video clips to help exemplify the words being learned.

Use the *Word List Data Sheet* that follows this story to track a learner's progress.

Use the *Master Word List Data Sheet* in the Appendix to track word recognition mastery.

**Note:** Words appearing in previous stories are regarded as being familiar to the learner. However, some review may be necessary to maintain word recognition and understanding.

# A number of children will come to watch the parade. They love the floats the people made.

# Word List Data Sheets

**(Copy this sheet as often as necessary to track progress over time)**

| Date: | Some Assistance | No Assistance | Date: | Some Assistance | No Assistance | Date: | Some Assistance | No Assistance | Date: | Some Assistance | No Assistance |
|---|---|---|---|---|---|---|---|---|---|---|---|
| | | | | | | | | | | | |
| | | | | | | | | | | | |
| | | | | | | | | | | | |
| | | | | | | | | | | | |
| | | | | | | | | | | | |
| | | | | | | | | | | | |
| | | | | | | | | | | | |
| | | | | | | | | | | | |
| | | | | | | | | | | | |
| | | | | | | | | | | | |

**Reading With Ease: An Alternative Method, Series 1, Volume 1**

# Story 10

there
are
yellow
flowers
garden
how
if
could
would
this

# Tips for the Reading Facilitator:

Using a sheet of paper, cover all lines/sentences below the line/sentence the learner will read. Once the learner has read the line/sentence (with assistance or independently), uncover the next line/sentence. This technique offers less distraction and more focused attention on the line/sentence to be read.

After the learner reads each line/sentence (with or without assistance), provide positive reinforcement that is meaningful to the learner.
Be creative, use objects or video clips to help exemplify the words being learned.

Use the *Word List Data Sheet* that follows this story to track a learner's progress.

Use the *Master Word List Data Sheet* in the Appendix to track word recognition mastery.

**Note:** Words appearing in previous stories are regarded as being familiar to the learner. However, some review may be necessary to maintain word recognition and understanding.

The story with word symbols begins on the next page.

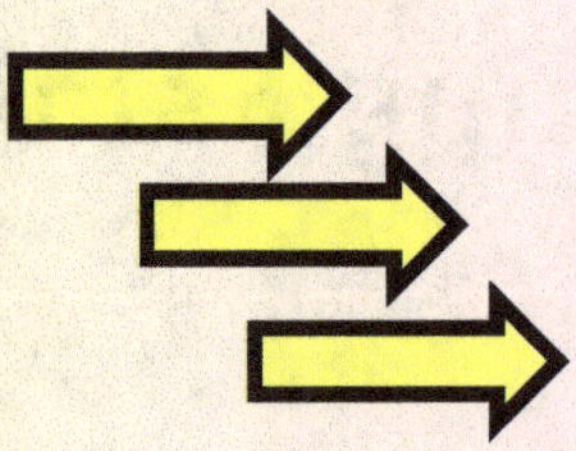

There   are   yellow   flowers

in   the   garden.

How   many   do   you   love ?

If   you   could,   would   you

play   in   this   garden   ?

# Tips for the Reading Facilitator:

Once the learner can fluently read the story with word symbols, have them read the same story shown on the next page which eliminates individual word symbols.

Using a sheet of paper, cover all lines/sentences below the line/sentence the learner will read. Once the learner has read the line/sentence (with assistance or independently), uncover the next line/sentence. This technique offers less distraction and more focused attention on the line/sentence to be read.

After the learner reads each line/sentence (with or without assistance), provide positive reinforcement that is meaningful to the learner.

Be creative, use objects or video clips to help exemplify the words being learned.

Use the *Word List Data Sheet* that follows this story to track a learner's progress.

Use the *Master Word List Data Sheet* in the Appendix to track word recognition mastery.

**Note:** Words appearing in previous stories are regarded as being familiar to the learner. However, some review may be necessary to maintain word recognition and understanding.

There are yellow flowers in the garden.

How many do you love?

If you could, would you play in this garden?

# Word List Data Sheets

**(Copy this sheet as often as necessary to track progress over time)**

| Date: | Some Assistance | No Assistance | Date: | Some Assistance | No Assistance | Date: | Some Assistance | No Assistance | Date: | Some Assistance | No Assistance |
|---|---|---|---|---|---|---|---|---|---|---|---|
| | | | | | | | | | | | |
| | | | | | | | | | | | |
| | | | | | | | | | | | |
| | | | | | | | | | | | |
| | | | | | | | | | | | |
| | | | | | | | | | | | |
| | | | | | | | | | | | |
| | | | | | | | | | | | |
| | | | | | | | | | | | |
| | | | | | | | | | | | |

# Story 11

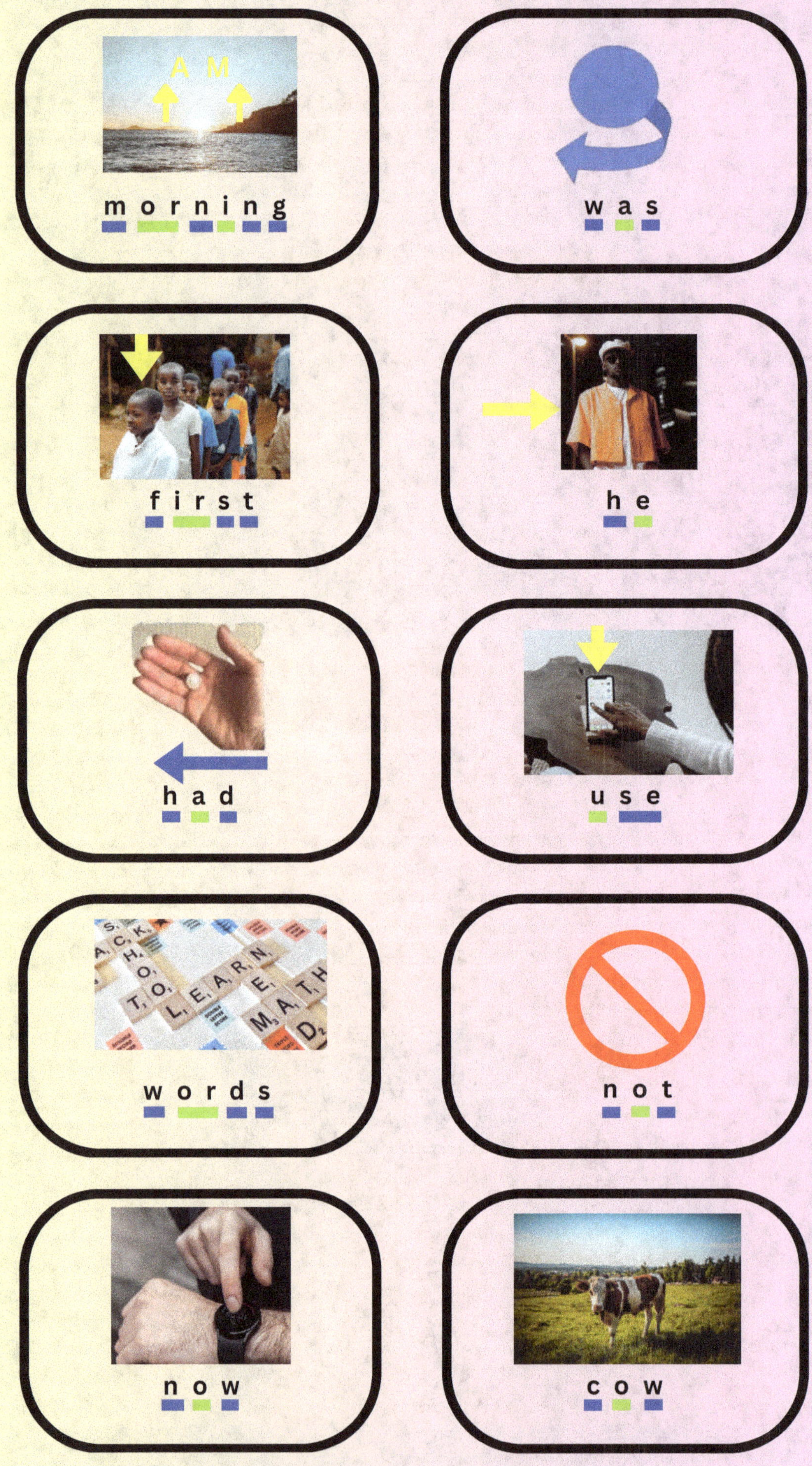
A M
morning
was
first
he
had
use
words
not
now
cow

# Tips for the Reading Facilitator:

Using a sheet of paper, cover all lines/sentences below the line/sentence the learner will read. Once the learner has read the line/sentence (with assistance or independently), uncover the next line/sentence. This technique offers less distraction and more focused attention on the line/sentence to be read.

After the learner reads each line/sentence (with or without assistance), provide positive reinforcement that is meaningful to the learner.
Be creative, use objects or video clips to help exemplify the words being learned.

Use the *Word List Data Sheet* that follows this story to track a learner's progress.

Use the *Master Word List Data Sheet* in the Appendix to track word recognition mastery.

**Note:** Words appearing in previous stories are regarded as being familiar to the learner. However, some review may be necessary to maintain word recognition and understanding.

The story with word symbols begins on the next page.

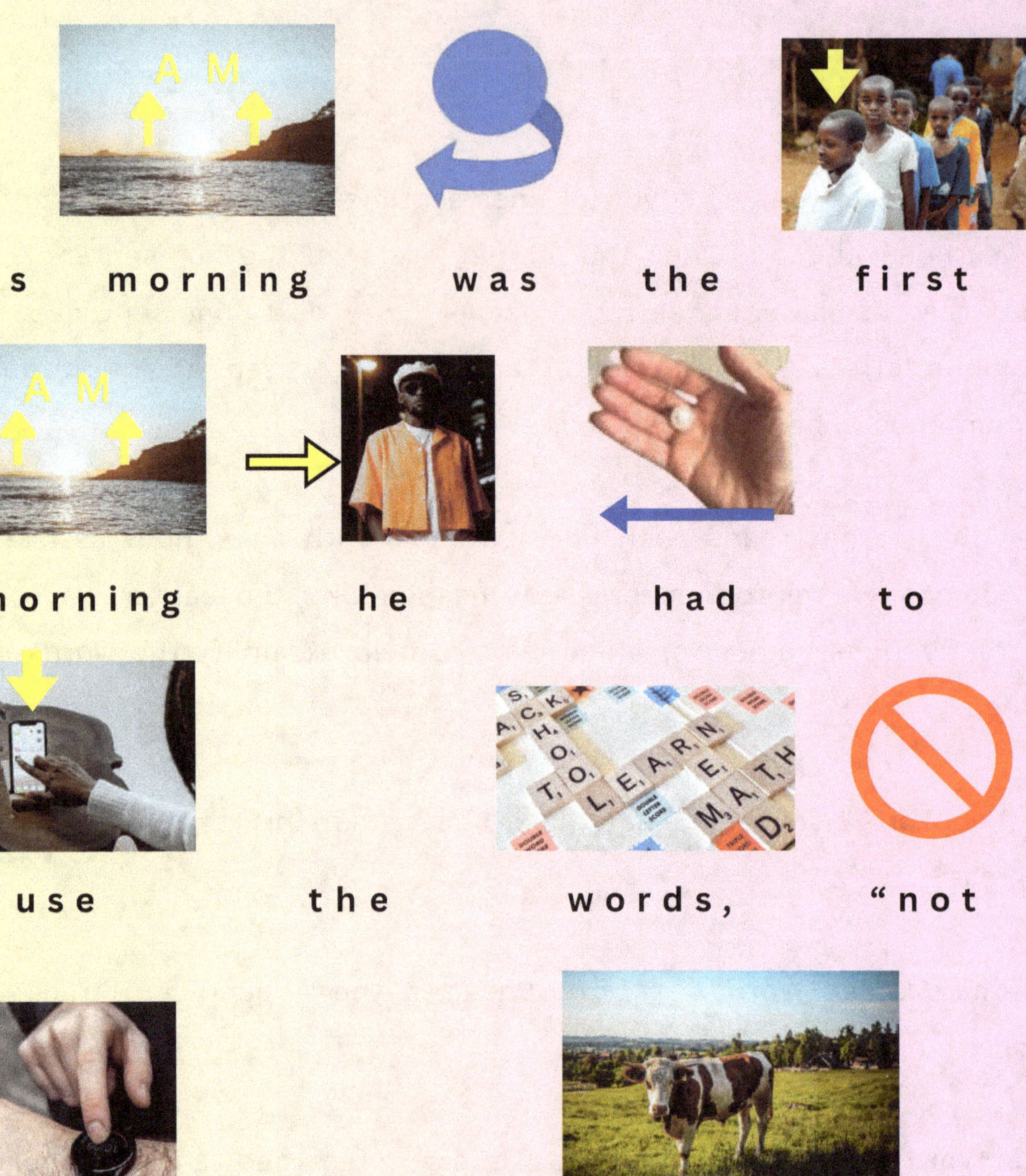

This   morning   was   the   first

morning   he   had   to

use   the   words,   "not

now"   to   the   cow.

# Tips for the Reading Facilitator:

Once the learner can fluently read the story with word symbols, have them read the same story shown on the next page which eliminates individual word symbols.

Using a sheet of paper, cover all lines/sentences below the line/sentence the learner will read. Once the learner has read the line/sentence (with assistance or independently), uncover the next line/sentence. This technique offers less distraction and more focused attention on the line/sentence to be read.

After the learner reads each line/sentence (with or without assistance), provide positive reinforcement that is meaningful to the learner.

Be creative, use objects or video clips to help exemplify the words being learned.

Use the *Word List Data Sheet* that follows this story to track a learner's progress.

Use the *Master Word List Data Sheet* in the Appendix to track word recognition mastery.

**Note:** Words appearing in previous stories are regarded as being familiar to the learner. However, some review may be necessary to maintain word recognition and understanding.

# This morning was the first morning he had to use the words, "not now" to the cow.

# Word List Data Sheets

**(Copy this sheet as often as necessary to track progress over time)**

| Date: | Some Assistance | No Assistance | Date: | Some Assistance | No Assistance | Date: | Some Assistance | No Assistance | Date: | Some Assistance | No Assistance |
|---|---|---|---|---|---|---|---|---|---|---|---|
| | | | | | | | | | | | |
| | | | | | | | | | | | |
| | | | | | | | | | | | |
| | | | | | | | | | | | |
| | | | | | | | | | | | |
| | | | | | | | | | | | |
| | | | | | | | | | | | |
| | | | | | | | | | | | |
| | | | | | | | | | | | |
| | | | | | | | | | | | |

**Reading With Ease: An Alternative Method, Series 1, Volume 1**

# Story 12

when
went
duck
farm
did
enjoy
charm
look
at
ducks

# Tips for the Reading Facilitator:

Using a sheet of paper, cover all lines/sentences below the line/sentence the learner will read. Once the learner has read the line/sentence (with assistance or independently), uncover the next line/sentence. This technique offers less distraction and more focused attention on the line/sentence to be read.

After the learner reads each line/sentence (with or without assistance), provide positive reinforcement that is meaningful to the learner.
Be creative, use objects or video clips to help exemplify the words being learned.

Use the *Word List Data Sheet* that follows this story to track a learner's progress.

Use the *Master Word List Data Sheet* in the Appendix to track word recognition mastery.

**Note:** Words appearing in previous stories are regarded as being familiar to the learner. However, some review may be necessary to maintain word recognition and understanding.

The story with word symbols begins on the next page.

**When we went to the**

**duck farm we did enjoy**

**its charm.**

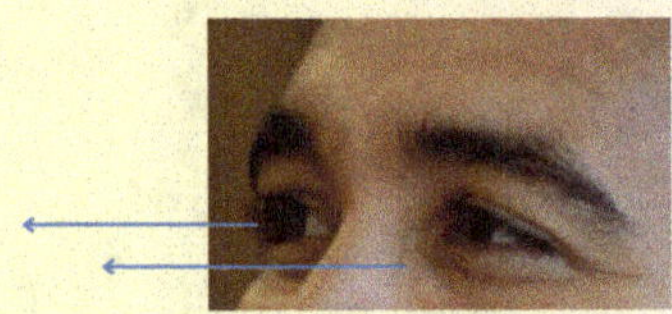   

**Look at all the ducks !**

# Tips for the Reading Facilitator:

Once the learner can fluently read the story with word symbols, have them read the same story shown on the next page which eliminates individual word symbols.

Using a sheet of paper, cover all lines/sentences below the line/sentence the learner will read. Once the learner has read the line/sentence (with assistance or independently), uncover the next line/sentence. This technique offers less distraction and more focused attention on the line/sentence to be read.

After the learner reads each line/sentence (with or without assistance), provide positive reinforcement that is meaningful to the learner.

Be creative, use objects or video clips to help exemplify the words being learned.

Use the *Word List Data Sheet* that follows this story to track a learner's progress.

Use the *Master Word List Data Sheet* in the Appendix to track word recognition mastery.

**Note:** Words appearing in previous stories are regarded as being familiar to the learner. However, some review may be necessary to maintain word recognition and understanding.

When we went to the
duck farm we did enjoy
its charm.

Look at all the ducks!

# Word List Data Sheets

**(Copy this sheet as often as necessary to track progress over time)**

| Date: | Some Assistance | No Assistance | Date: | Some Assistance | No Assistance | Date: | Some Assistance | No Assistance | Date: | Some Assistance | No Assistance |
|---|---|---|---|---|---|---|---|---|---|---|---|
| | | | | | | | | | | | |
| | | | | | | | | | | | |
| | | | | | | | | | | | |
| | | | | | | | | | | | |
| | | | | | | | | | | | |
| | | | | | | | | | | | |
| | | | | | | | | | | | |
| | | | | | | | | | | | |
| | | | | | | | | | | | |

**Reading With Ease: An Alternative Method, Series 1, Volume 1**

# Story 13

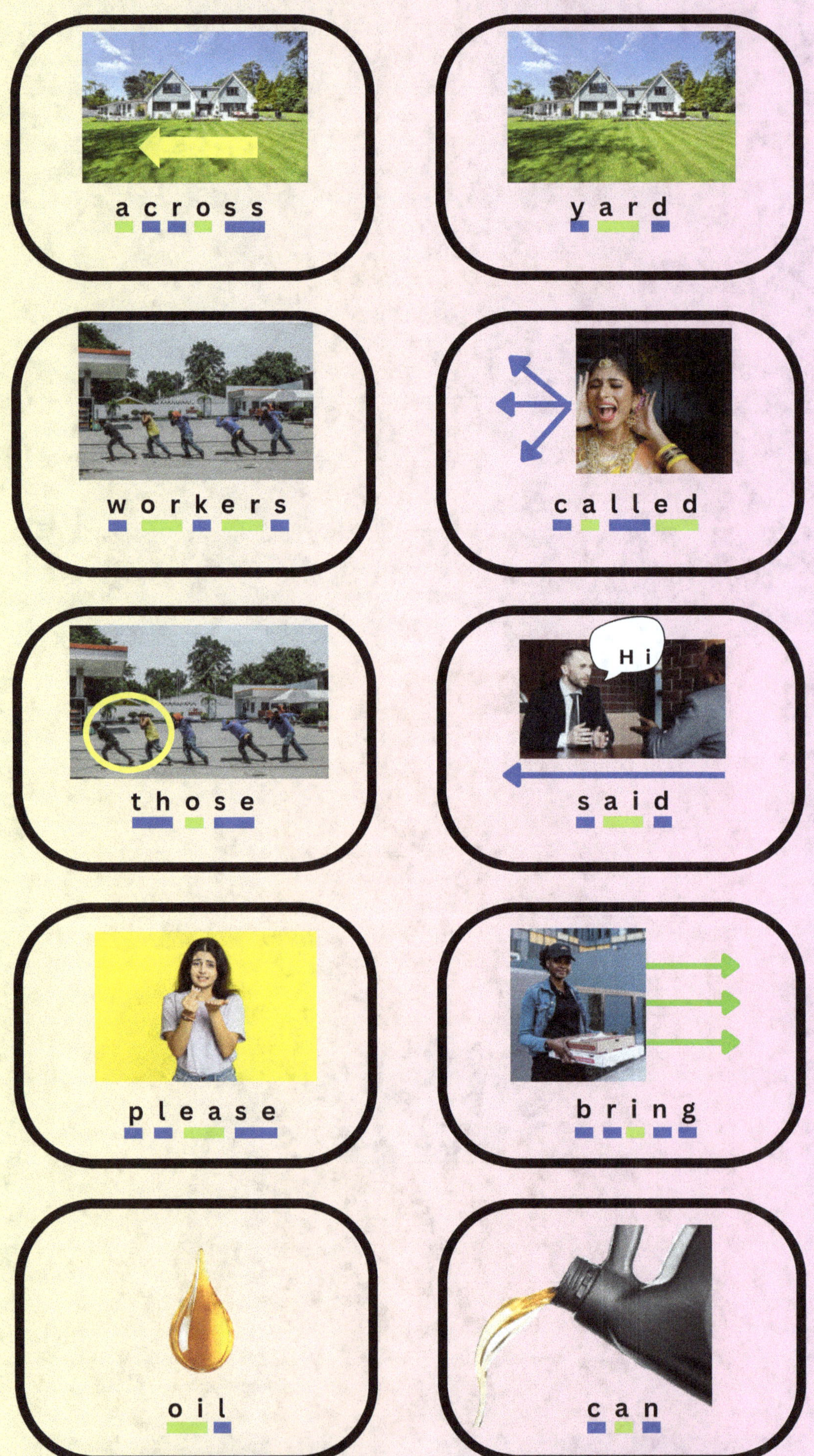
across
yard
workers
called
those
Hi
said
please
bring
oil
can

# Tips for the Reading Facilitator:

Using a sheet of paper, cover all lines/sentences below the line/sentence the learner will read. Once the learner has read the line/sentence (with assistance or independently), uncover the next line/sentence. This technique offers less distraction and more focused attention on the line/sentence to be read.

After the learner reads each line/sentence (with or without assistance), provide positive reinforcement that is meaningful to the learner.
Be creative, use objects or video clips to help exemplify the words being learned.

Use the *Word List Data Sheet* that follows this story to track a learner's progress.

Use the *Master Word List Data Sheet* in the Appendix to track word recognition mastery.

**Note:** Words appearing in previous stories are regarded as being familiar to the learner. However, some review may be necessary to maintain word recognition and understanding.

The story with word symbols begins on the next page.

From across the yard, he

called to those workers.

He said, "Please bring me

my oil can."

# Tips for the Reading Facilitator:

Once the learner can fluently read the story with word symbols, have them read the same story shown on the next page which eliminates individual word symbols.

Using a sheet of paper, cover all lines/sentences below the line/sentence the learner will read. Once the learner has read the line/sentence (with assistance or independently), uncover the next line/sentence. This technique offers less distraction and more focused attention on the line/sentence to be read.

After the learner reads each line/sentence (with or without assistance), provide positive reinforcement that is meaningful to the learner.

Be creative, use objects or video clips to help exemplify the words being learned.

Use the *Word List Data Sheet* that follows this story to track a learner's progress.

Use the *Master Word List Data Sheet* in the Appendix to track word recognition mastery.

**Note:** Words appearing in previous stories are regarded as being familiar to the learner. However, some review may be necessary to maintain word recognition and understanding.

From across the yard, he called to those workers. He said, "Please bring me my oil can."

# Word List Data Sheets

**(Copy this sheet as often as necessary to track progress over time)**

| Date: | | | Date: | | | Date: | | | Date: | | |
|---|---|---|---|---|---|---|---|---|---|---|---|
| Assistance | Some Assistance | No Assistance | Assistance | Some Assistance | No Assistance | Assistance | Some Assistance | No Assistance | Assistance | Some Assistance | No Assistance |
| | | | | | | | | | | | |
| | | | | | | | | | | | |
| | | | | | | | | | | | |
| | | | | | | | | | | | |
| | | | | | | | | | | | |
| | | | | | | | | | | | |
| | | | | | | | | | | | |
| | | | | | | | | | | | |
| | | | | | | | | | | | |

# Story 14

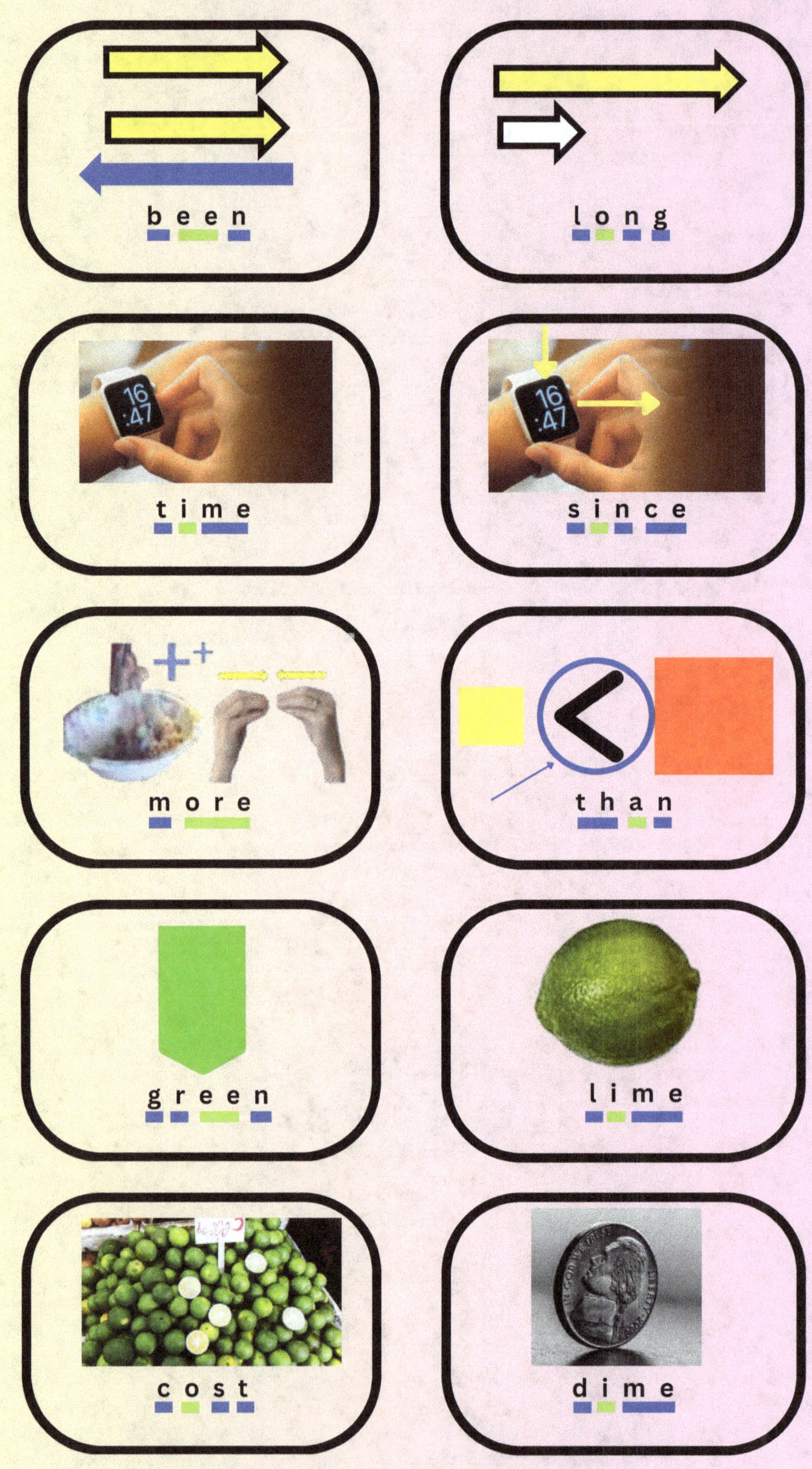


been
long
time
since
more
than
green
lime
cost
dime

# Tips for the Reading Facilitator:

Using a sheet of paper, cover all lines/sentences below the line/sentence the learner will read. Once the learner has read the line/sentence (with assistance or independently), uncover the next line/sentence. This technique offers less distraction and more focused attention on the line/sentence to be read.

After the learner reads each line/sentence (with or without assistance), provide positive reinforcement that is meaningful to the learner.
Be creative, use objects or video clips to help exemplify the words being learned.

Use the *Word List Data Sheet* that follows this story to track a learner's progress.

Use the *Master Word List Data Sheet* in the Appendix to track word recognition mastery.

**Note:** Words appearing in previous stories are regarded as being familiar to the learner. However, some review may be necessary to maintain word recognition and understanding.

The story with word symbols begins on the next page.

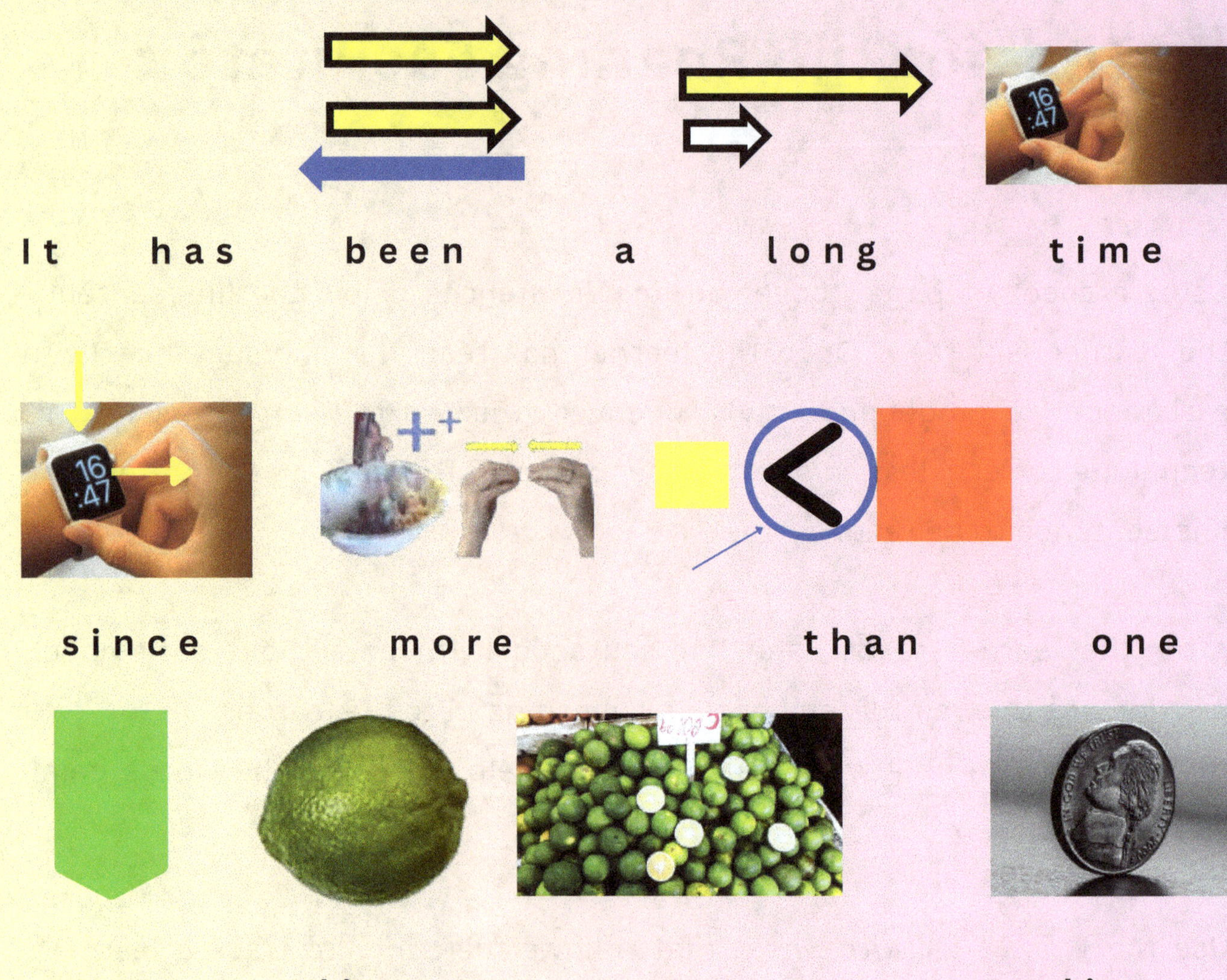

It   has   been   a   long   time

since   more   than   one

green   lime   cost   a   dime.

# Tips for the Reading Facilitator:

Once the learner can fluently read the story with word symbols, have them read the same story shown on the next page which eliminates individual word symbols.

Using a sheet of paper, cover all lines/sentences below the line/sentence the learner will read. Once the learner has read the line/sentence (with assistance or independently), uncover the next line/sentence. This technique offers less distraction and more focused attention on the line/sentence to be read.

After the learner reads each line/sentence (with or without assistance), provide positive reinforcement that is meaningful to the learner.

Be creative, use objects or video clips to help exemplify the words being learned.

Use the *Word List Data Sheet* that follows this story to track a learner's progress.

Use the *Master Word List Data Sheet* in the Appendix to track word recognition mastery.

**Note:** Words appearing in previous stories are regarded as being familiar to the learner. However, some review may be necessary to maintain word recognition and understanding.

It has been a long time since more than one green lime cost a dime.

# Word List Data Sheets

**(Copy this sheet as often as necessary to track progress over time)**

| Date: | | | Date: | | | Date: | | | Date: | | |
|---|---|---|---|---|---|---|---|---|---|---|---|
| | Some Assistance | No Assistance | Assistance | Some Assistance | No Assistance | Assistance | Some Assistance | No Assistance | Assistance | Some Assistance | No Assistance |
| | | | | | | | | | | | |
| | | | | | | | | | | | |
| | | | | | | | | | | | |
| | | | | | | | | | | | |
| | | | | | | | | | | | |
| | | | | | | | | | | | |
| | | | | | | | | | | | |
| | | | | | | | | | | | |
| | | | | | | | | | | | |

**Reading With Ease: An Alternative Method, Series 1, Volume 1**

# Story 15

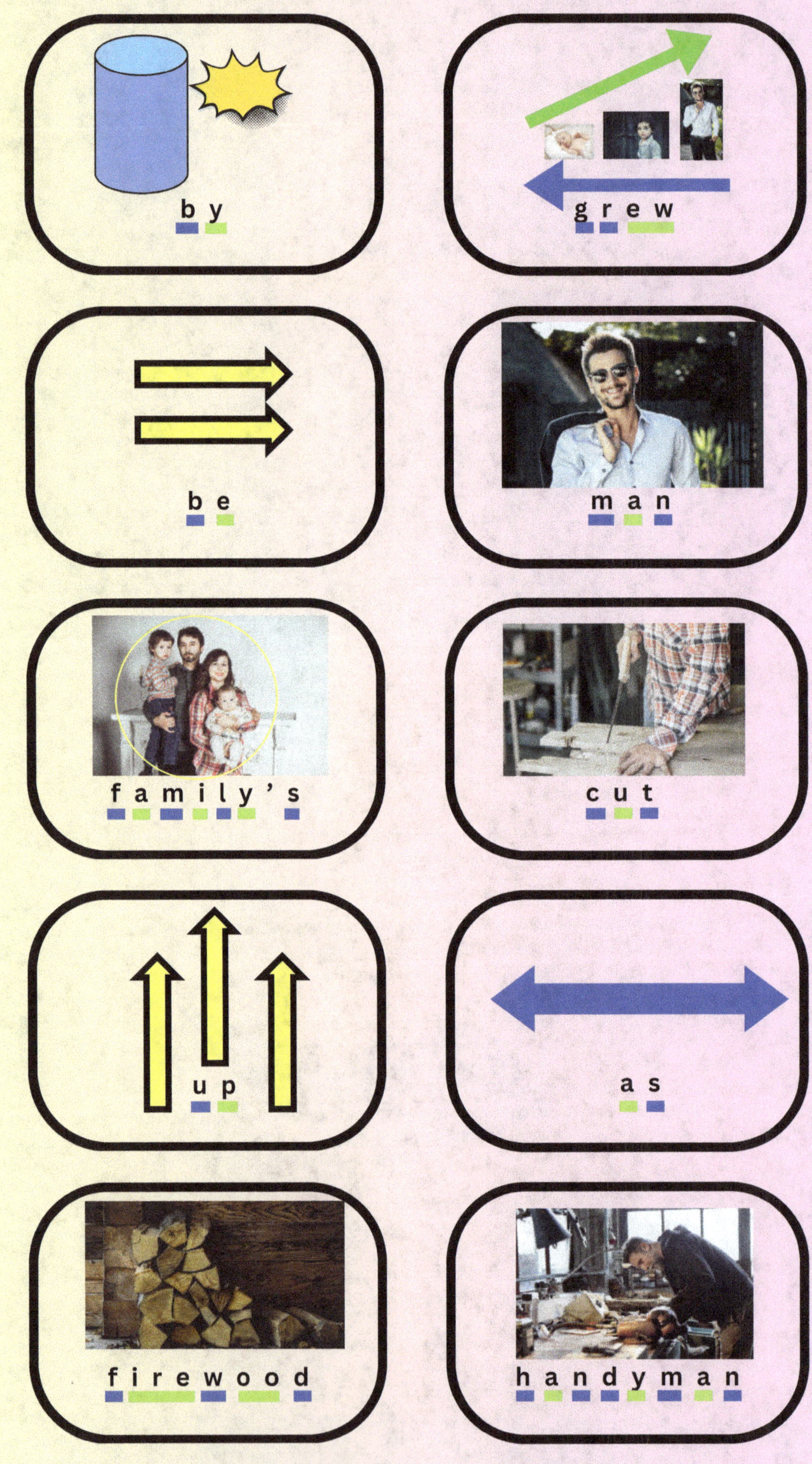
by
grew
be
man
family's
cut
up
as
firewood
handyman

# Tips for the Reading Facilitator:

Using a sheet of paper, cover all lines/sentences below the line/sentence the learner will read. Once the learner has read the line/sentence (with assistance or independently), uncover the next line/sentence. This technique offers less distraction and more focused attention on the line/sentence to be read.

After the learner reads each line/sentence (with or without assistance), provide positive reinforcement that is meaningful to the learner.
Be creative, use objects or video clips to help exemplify the words being learned.

Use the *Word List Data Sheet* that follows this story to track a learner's progress.

Use the *Master Word List Data Sheet* in the Appendix to track word recognition mastery.

**Note:** Words appearing in previous stories are regarded as being familiar to the learner. However, some review may be necessary to maintain word recognition and understanding.

The story with word symbols begins on the next page.

By the time he grew to

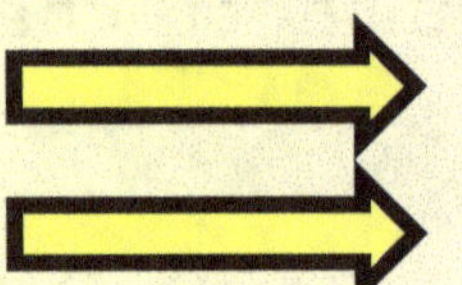  

be a man, his family's tree

 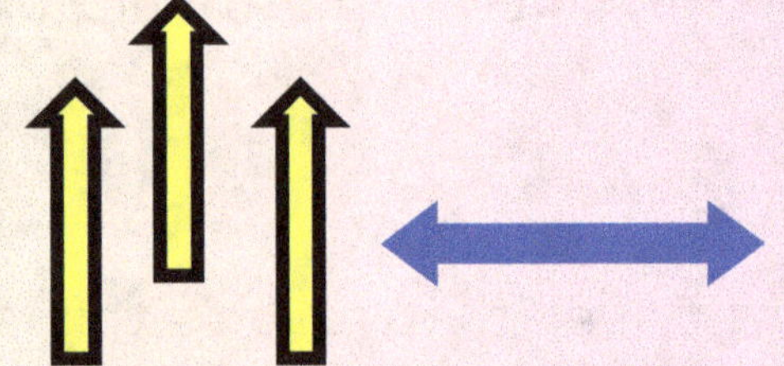 

was cut up as firewood

by a handyman.

# Tips for the Reading Facilitator:

Once the learner can fluently read the story with word symbols, have them read the same story shown on the next page which eliminates individual word symbols.

Using a sheet of paper, cover all lines/sentences below the line/sentence the learner will read. Once the learner has read the line/sentence (with assistance or independently), uncover the next line/sentence. This technique offers less distraction and more focused attention on the line/sentence to be read.

After the learner reads each line/sentence (with or without assistance), provide positive reinforcement that is meaningful to the learner.

Be creative, use objects or video clips to help exemplify the words being learned.

Use the *Word List Data Sheet* that follows this story to track a learner's progress.

Use the *Master Word List Data Sheet* in the Appendix to track word recognition mastery.

**Note:** Words appearing in previous stories are regarded as being familiar to the learner. However, some review may be necessary to maintain word recognition and understanding.

By the time he grew to be a man, his family's tree was cut up as firewood by a handyman.

# Word List Data Sheets

**(Copy this sheet as often as necessary to track progress over time)**

| Date: | | | Date: | | | Date: | | | Date: | | |
|---|---|---|---|---|---|---|---|---|---|---|---|
| Assistance | Some Assistance | No Assistance | Assistance | Some Assistance | No Assistance | Assistance | Some Assistance | No Assistance | Assistance | Some Assistance | No Assistance |
| | | | | | | | | | | | |
| | | | | | | | | | | | |
| | | | | | | | | | | | |
| | | | | | | | | | | | |
| | | | | | | | | | | | |
| | | | | | | | | | | | |
| | | | | | | | | | | | |
| | | | | | | | | | | | |
| | | | | | | | | | | | |
| | | | | | | | | | | | |

**Reading With Ease: An Alternative Method, Series 1, Volume 1**

# Story 16

each
drop
rain
or
snowflake
falls
down
cloud
which
plowed

# Tips for the Reading Facilitator:

Using a sheet of paper, cover all lines/sentences below the line/sentence the learner will read. Once the learner has read the line/sentence (with assistance or independently), uncover the next line/sentence. This technique offers less distraction and more focused attention on the line/sentence to be read.

After the learner reads each line/sentence (with or without assistance), provide positive reinforcement that is meaningful to the learner.
Be creative, use objects or video clips to help exemplify the words being learned.

Use the *Word List Data Sheet* that follows this story to track a learner's progress.

Use the *Master Word List Data Sheet* in the Appendix to track word recognition mastery.

**Note:** Words appearing in previous stories are regarded as being familiar to the learner. However, some review may be necessary to maintain word recognition and understanding.

The story with word symbols begins on the next page.

Each     drop     of     rain

or          snowflake          falls

down     from     a     cloud.

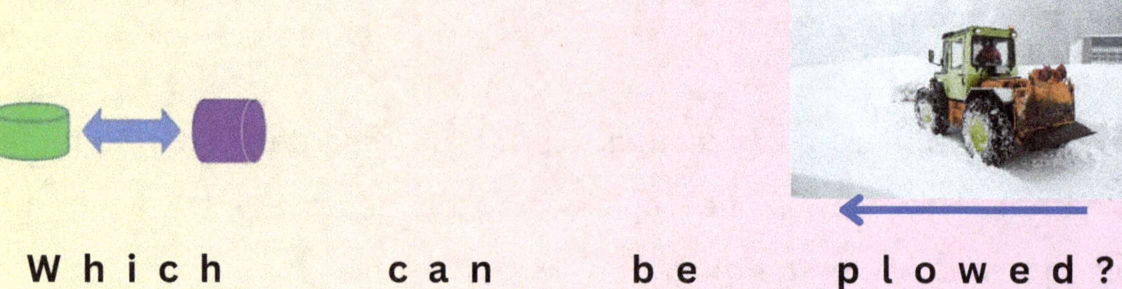

Which          can          be          plowed?

# Tips for the Reading Facilitator:

Once the learner can fluently read the story with word symbols, have them read the same story shown on the next page which eliminates individual word symbols.

Using a sheet of paper, cover all lines/sentences below the line/sentence the learner will read. Once the learner has read the line/sentence (with assistance or independently), uncover the next line/sentence. This technique offers less distraction and more focused attention on the line/sentence to be read.

After the learner reads each line/sentence (with or without assistance), provide positive reinforcement that is meaningful to the learner.

Be creative, use objects or video clips to help exemplify the words being learned.

Use the *Word List Data Sheet* that follows this story to track a learner's progress.

Use the *Master Word List Data Sheet* in the Appendix to track word recognition mastery.

**Note:** Words appearing in previous stories are regarded as being familiar to the learner. However, some review may be necessary to maintain word recognition and understanding.

# Each drop of rain or snowflake falls down from a cloud.

# Which can be plowed?

# Word List Data Sheets

**(Copy this sheet as often as necessary to track progress over time)**

| Date: | Some Assistance | No Assistance | Date: | Some Assistance | No Assistance | Date: | Some Assistance | No Assistance | Date: | Some Assistance | No Assistance |
|---|---|---|---|---|---|---|---|---|---|---|---|
| | | | | | | | | | | | |
| | | | | | | | | | | | |
| | | | | | | | | | | | |
| | | | | | | | | | | | |
| | | | | | | | | | | | |
| | | | | | | | | | | | |
| | | | | | | | | | | | |
| | | | | | | | | | | | |
| | | | | | | | | | | | |

**Reading With Ease: An Alternative Method, Series 1, Volume 1**

# Story 17

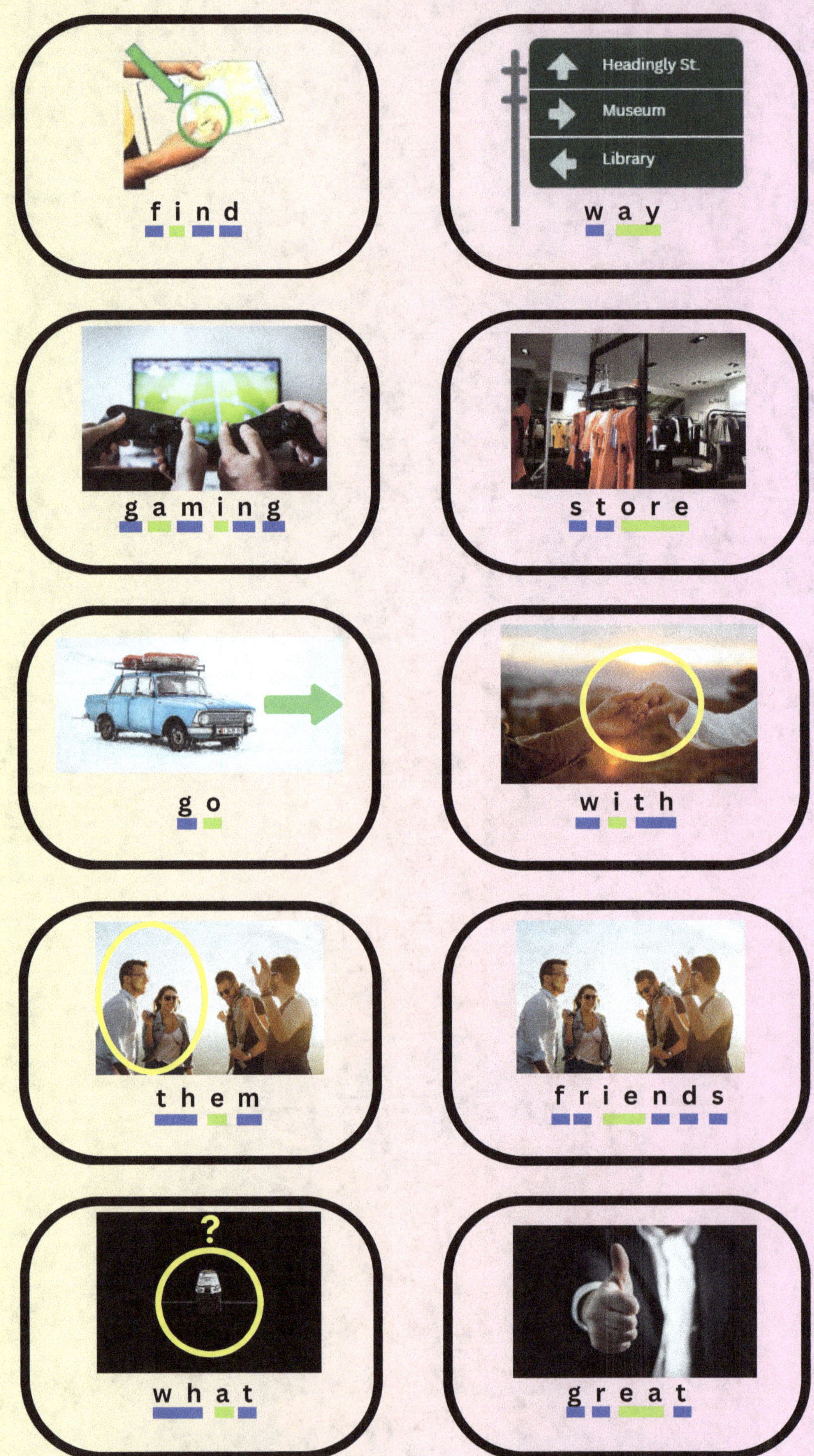
find
way
gaming
store
go
with
them
friends
what
great

# Tips for the Reading Facilitator:

Using a sheet of paper, cover all lines/sentences below the line/sentence the learner will read. Once the learner has read the line/sentence (with assistance or independently), uncover the next line/sentence. This technique offers less distraction and more focused attention on the line/sentence to be read.

After the learner reads each line/sentence (with or without assistance), provide positive reinforcement that is meaningful to the learner.
Be creative, use objects or video clips to help exemplify the words being learned.

Use the *Word List Data Sheet* that follows this story to track a learner's progress.

Use the *Master Word List Data Sheet* in the Appendix to track word recognition mastery.

**Note:** Words appearing in previous stories are regarded as being familiar to the learner. However, some review may be necessary to maintain word recognition and understanding.

The story with word symbols begins on the next page.

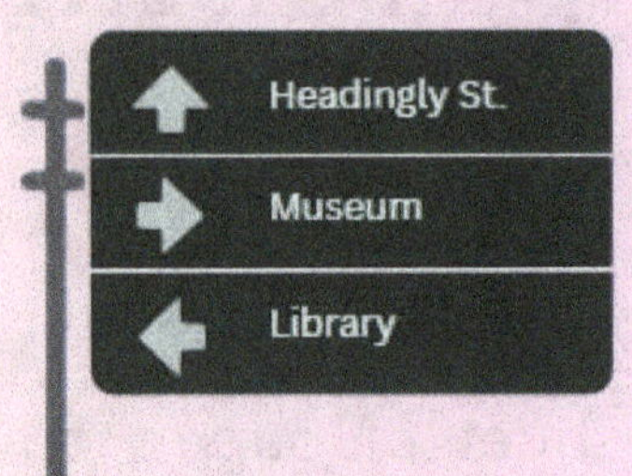


He  will  find  his  way

to  the  gaming  store.

He  will  go  with

them,  his  friends.

What  a  great  day!

# Tips for the Reading Facilitator:

Once the learner can fluently read the story with word symbols, have them read the same story shown on the next page which eliminates individual word symbols.

Using a sheet of paper, cover all lines/sentences below the line/sentence the learner will read. Once the learner has read the line/sentence (with assistance or independently), uncover the next line/sentence. This technique offers less distraction and more focused attention on the line/sentence to be read.

After the learner reads each line/sentence (with or without assistance), provide positive reinforcement that is meaningful to the learner.

Be creative, use objects or video clips to help exemplify the words being learned.

Use the *Word List Data Sheet* that follows this story to track a learner's progress.

Use the *Master Word List Data Sheet* in the Appendix to track word recognition mastery.

**Note:** Words appearing in previous stories are regarded as being familiar to the learner. However, some review may be necessary to maintain word recognition and understanding.

He will find his way to the gaming store. He will go with them, his friends.

What a great day!

# Word List Data Sheets

**(Copy this sheet as often as necessary to track progress over time)**

| Date: | Some Assistance | No Assistance | Date: | Some Assistance | No Assistance | Date: | Some Assistance | No Assistance | Date: | Some Assistance | No Assistance |
|---|---|---|---|---|---|---|---|---|---|---|---|
| | | | | | | | | | | | |
| | | | | | | | | | | | |
| | | | | | | | | | | | |
| | | | | | | | | | | | |
| | | | | | | | | | | | |
| | | | | | | | | | | | |
| | | | | | | | | | | | |
| | | | | | | | | | | | |
| | | | | | | | | | | | |
| | | | | | | | | | | | |

**Reading With Ease: An Alternative Method, Series 1, Volume 1**

# Story 18

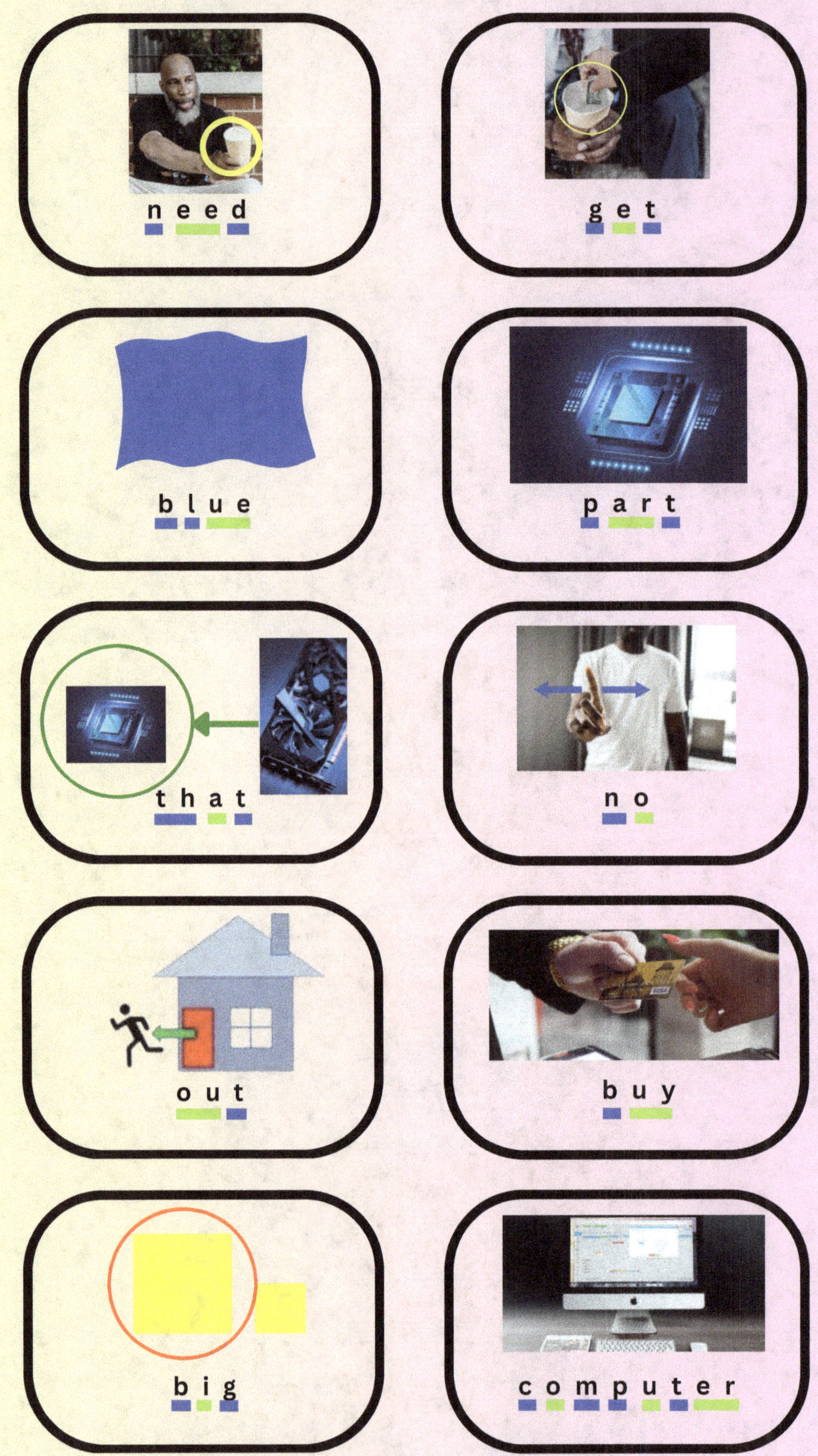

need
get
blue
part
that
no
out
buy
big
computer

# Tips for the Reading Facilitator:

Using a sheet of paper, cover all lines/sentences below the line/sentence the learner will read. Once the learner has read the line/sentence (with assistance or independently), uncover the next line/sentence. This technique offers less distraction and more focused attention on the line/sentence to be read.

After the learner reads each line/sentence (with or without assistance), provide positive reinforcement that is meaningful to the learner.
Be creative, use objects or video clips to help exemplify the words being learned.

Use the *Word List Data Sheet* that follows this story to track a learner's progress.

Use the *Master Word List Data Sheet* in the Appendix to track word recognition mastery.

**Note:** Words appearing in previous stories are regarded as being familiar to the learner. However, some review may be necessary to maintain word recognition and understanding.

The story with word symbols begins on the next page.

Who will get the blue

 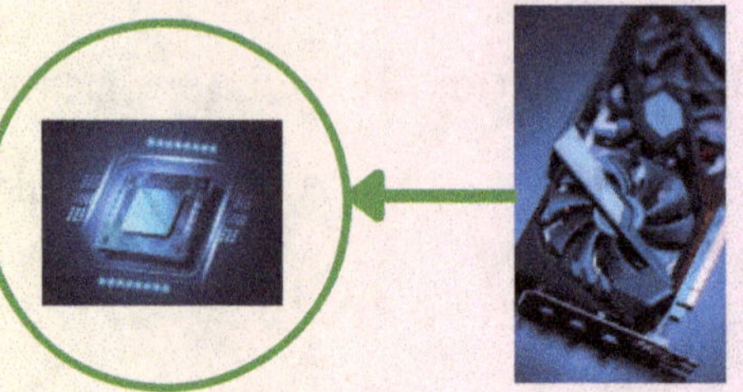 

part that we need

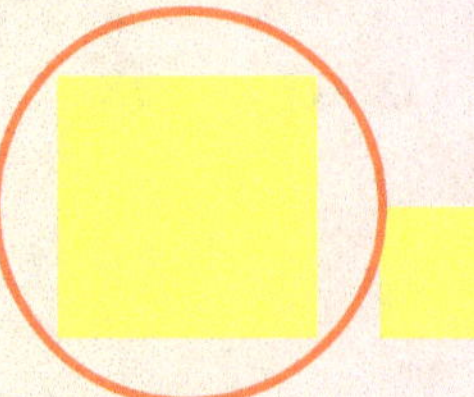 

for the big computer ?

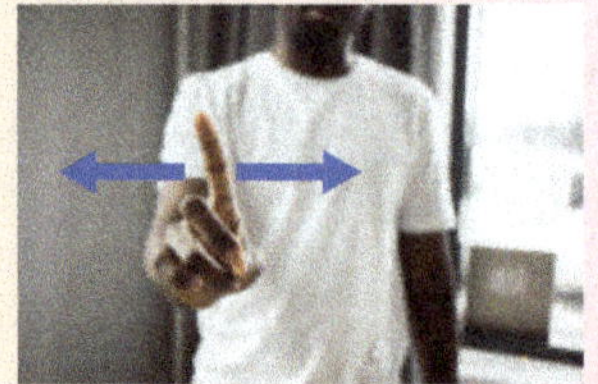

He said, "no".

So, will you go out to buy it?

# Tips for the Reading Facilitator:

Once the learner can fluently read the story with word symbols, have them read the same story shown on the next page which eliminates individual word symbols.

Using a sheet of paper, cover all lines/sentences below the line/sentence the learner will read. Once the learner has read the line/sentence (with assistance or independently), uncover the next line/sentence. This technique offers less distraction and more focused attention on the line/sentence to be read.

After the learner reads each line/sentence (with or without assistance), provide positive reinforcement that is meaningful to the learner.

Be creative, use objects or video clips to help exemplify the words being learned.

Use the *Word List Data Sheet* that follows this story to track a learner's progress.

Use the *Master Word List Data Sheet* in the Appendix to track word recognition mastery.

**Note:** Words appearing in previous stories are regarded as being familiar to the learner. However, some review may be necessary to maintain word recognition and understanding.

Who will get the blue part that we need for the big computer?

He said, "no".

So, will you go out to buy it?

# Word List Data Sheets

**(Copy this sheet as often as necessary to track progress over time)**

| Date: | Some Assistance | No Assistance | Date: | Some Assistance | No Assistance | Date: | Some Assistance | No Assistance | Date: | Some Assistance | No Assistance |
|---|---|---|---|---|---|---|---|---|---|---|---|
| | | | | | | | | | | | |
| | | | | | | | | | | | |
| | | | | | | | | | | | |
| | | | | | | | | | | | |
| | | | | | | | | | | | |
| | | | | | | | | | | | |
| | | | | | | | | | | | |
| | | | | | | | | | | | |
| | | | | | | | | | | | |
| | | | | | | | | | | | |

**Reading With Ease: An Alternative Method, Series 1, Volume 1**

# Story 19

funny
Hi
tell
loudly
3
three
I need water.
help
run
jump
away
here
little

# Tips for the Reading Facilitator:

Using a sheet of paper, cover all lines/sentences below the line/sentence the learner will read. Once the learner has read the line/sentence (with assistance or independently), uncover the next line/sentence. This technique offers less distraction and more focused attention on the line/sentence to be read.

After the learner reads each line/sentence (with or without assistance), provide positive reinforcement that is meaningful to the learner.
Be creative, use objects or video clips to help exemplify the words being learned.

Use the *Word List Data Sheet* that follows this story to track a learner's progress.

Use the *Master Word List Data Sheet* in the Appendix to track word recognition mastery.

**Note:** Words appearing in previous stories are regarded as being familiar to the learner. However, some review may be necessary to maintain word recognition and understanding.

The story with word symbols begins on the next page.

Elaine M. Peters

I   love   when   my   three   friends

are   here   with   me.

They   tell   me   funny   stories

that   make   me   laugh   loudly.

They   help   me   run   and   jump.

The   little   time   they   are   away,
I   do   not   go   out.

# Tips for the Reading Facilitator:

Once the learner can fluently read the story with word symbols, have them read the same story shown on the next page which eliminates individual word symbols.

Using a sheet of paper, cover all lines/sentences below the line/sentence the learner will read. Once the learner has read the line/sentence (with assistance or independently), uncover the next line/sentence. This technique offers less distraction and more focused attention on the line/sentence to be read.

After the learner reads each line/sentence (with or without assistance), provide positive reinforcement that is meaningful to the learner.

Be creative, use objects or video clips to help exemplify the words being learned.

Use the *Word List Data Sheet* that follows this story to track a learner's progress.

Use the *Master Word List Data Sheet* in the Appendix to track word recognition mastery.

**Note:** Words appearing in previous stories are regarded as being familiar to the learner. However, some review may be necessary to maintain word recognition and understanding.

I love when my three friends are here with me.

They tell me funny stories that make me laugh loudly.

They help me run and jump.

The little time they are away, I do not go out.

# Word List Data Sheets

**(Copy this sheet as often as necessary to track progress over time)**

| Date: | | | Date: | | | Date: | | | Date: | | |
|---|---|---|---|---|---|---|---|---|---|---|---|
| Assistance | Some Assistance | No Assistance | Assistance | Some Assistance | No Assistance | Assistance | Some Assistance | No Assistance | Assistance | Some Assistance | No Assistance |
| | | | | | | | | | | | |
| | | | | | | | | | | | |
| | | | | | | | | | | | |
| | | | | | | | | | | | |
| | | | | | | | | | | | |
| | | | | | | | | | | | |
| | | | | | | | | | | | |
| | | | | | | | | | | | |
| | | | | | | | | | | | |
| | | | | | | | | | | | |

**Reading With Ease: An Alternative Method, Series 1, Volume 1**

# Story 20

am
full
ate
black
rice
came
must
try
our
favorite

# Tips for the Reading Facilitator:

Using a sheet of paper, cover all lines/sentences below the line/sentence the learner will read. Once the learner has read the line/sentence (with assistance or independently), uncover the next line/sentence. This technique offers less distraction and more focused attention on the line/sentence to be read.

After the learner reads each line/sentence (with or without assistance), provide positive reinforcement that is meaningful to the learner.
Be creative, use objects or video clips to help exemplify the words being learned.

Use the *Word List Data Sheet* that follows this story to track a learner's progress.

Use the *Master Word List Data Sheet* in the Appendix to track word recognition mastery.

**Note:** Words appearing in previous stories are regarded as being familiar to the learner. However, some review may be necessary to maintain word recognition and understanding.

The story with word symbols begins on the next page.

I  am  full.

   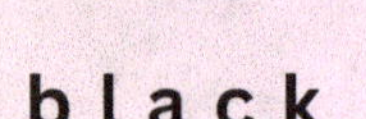 

I  ate  all  the  black  rice.

I  came  to  eat  it.

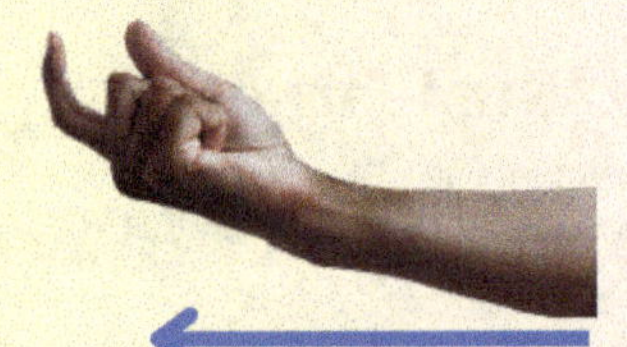 

My  friend  must  try  it.

It  will  be  our  favorite.

# Tips for the Reading Facilitator:

Once the learner can fluently read the story with word symbols, have them read the same story shown on the next page which eliminates individual word symbols.

Using a sheet of paper, cover all lines/sentences below the line/sentence the learner will read. Once the learner has read the line/sentence (with assistance or independently), uncover the next line/sentence. This technique offers less distraction and more focused attention on the line/sentence to be read.

After the learner reads each line/sentence (with or without assistance), provide positive reinforcement that is meaningful to the learner.

Be creative, use objects or video clips to help exemplify the words being learned.

Use the *Word List Data Sheet* that follows this story to track a learner's progress.

Use the *Master Word List Data Sheet* in the Appendix to track word recognition mastery.

**Note:** Words appearing in previous stories are regarded as being familiar to the learner. However, some review may be necessary to maintain word recognition and understanding.

I am full.

I ate all the black rice.

I came to eat it.

My friend must try it.

It will be our favorite.

# Word List Data Sheets

**(Copy this sheet as often as necessary to track progress over time)**

| Date: | | | Date: | | | Date: | | | Date: | | |
|---|---|---|---|---|---|---|---|---|---|---|---|
| Assistance | Some Assistance | No Assistance | Assistance | Some Assistance | No Assistance | Assistance | Some Assistance | No Assistance | Assistance | Some Assistance | No Assistance |
| | | | | | | | | | | | |
| | | | | | | | | | | | |
| | | | | | | | | | | | |
| | | | | | | | | | | | |
| | | | | | | | | | | | |
| | | | | | | | | | | | |
| | | | | | | | | | | | |
| | | | | | | | | | | | |
| | | | | | | | | | | | |

**Reading With Ease: An Alternative Method, Series 1, Volume 1**

# Spelling Made Fun!

Congratulations!

The first level of reading based on the most frequent words in print (according to Dolch and Fry) is done. However, achieving mastery comes with practice. So, reading practice is worthwhile. Something to help achieve mastery is learning to spell each of the two hundred words in this alternative reading guide. Starting with the short words is best. However, following the interest of the learner is also best practice.

Here is an example of the procedure to encouraging spelling:

- The learner selects a word of interest.

- The facilitator (or the learner) prints each letter of the word on separate post-it notes. (Modification: The learner can use sheets of sticker alphabet letters, placing each letter of a word on separate post-it notes.) See Figure 1 on the next page.

- The facilitator scrambles the post-it notes.

- With the pictured word in sight, the facilitator demonstrates to the learner the procedure of unscrambling the letter post-it notes to match the letter order in the word of choice, phonetically pronouncing each letter as it is placed in sequence.

- The facilitator says to the learner. "Now it is your turn to place each letter in order matching the letter order of the word you chose."

- The facilitator may assist the learner's eye tracking using a pencil or other pointer type object to redirect as needed. Practice as many times as necessary to fade support until the learner is unscrambling the post-it note letters to spell the word independently.

- The last step is to remove the picture word card completely from view and have the learner unscramble the post-it notes' letters with phonetical assistance as needed. Practice until the learner is unscrambling the letters independently.

Give positive reinforcement to encourage further spelling ventures. Figure 1 below provides an example of this alternative learning to spell procedure.

Figure 1:

If an individual is interested in knowing more about the origins and/or definitions of any particular word, the facilitator can model how to search for the word using www.dictionary.com, a dictionary app, or a book style dictionary can be helpful. Encourage and support an individual's curiosity—it is the doorway to continuous, life-long learning.

**Noun Example**

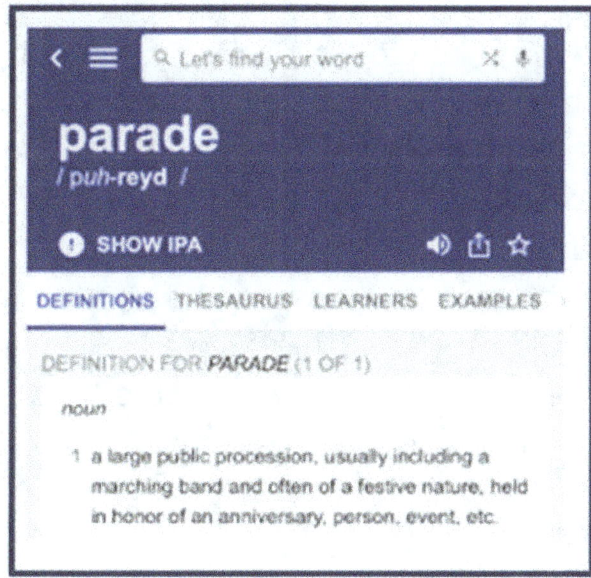


**Pronoun Example**

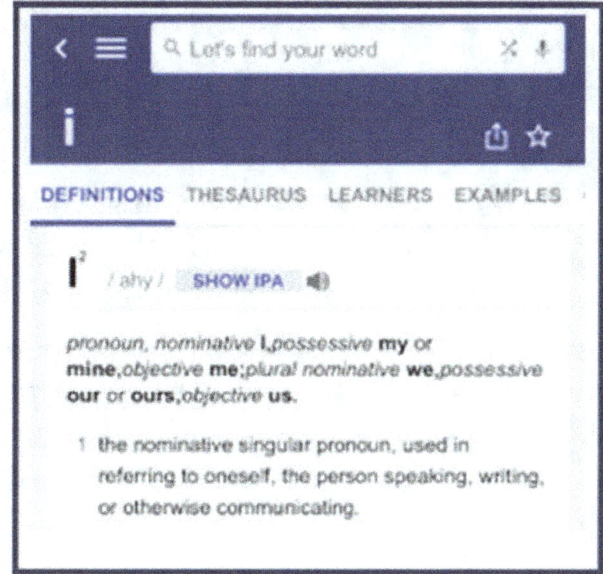

# Sentence Building
# (Mirroring)

Here is a fun way for an individual to practice building sentences:

- The individual chooses a story to use as the model for their sentence building.

- The individual chooses a sentence from within the model story to mirror.

- Gather all the Word Cards necessary for the individual to mirror the sentence from the model story chosen. Framing the selection of Word Cards is the best place to start (i.e., the facilitator assists the individual to select the Word Cards needed from a smaller pre-selected group of Word Cards). The goal: Over time and practice, the individual will be able to select Word Cards from among several more on their own.

- The individual builds a sentence that mirrors the sentence they chose from within the model story, with assistance as needed. Fade support and prompts gradually. NOTE: Fading support is the process of gradually reducing the quantity and type of support given to a learner to complete part of or all of a task or activity. The goal is for the learner to complete a task or activity independently.

An example of fading support is transitioning from hand-over-hand paired with verbal cues; to a light touch on the learner's elbow with verbal cues; to pointing with verbal cues; to verbal cues only; to pointing as needed only; to no prompts or cues at all.

- Practice this procedure for several more sentences until the individual demonstrates sentence mirroring mastery (i.e., no support or prompts are given by the facilitator).

# Sentence Building (Freestyle)

Enabling successful freestyle sentence building using Word Cards available from one or more stories within this facilitation guide requires backward planning. The facilitator, who has learned which words the learner knows well, begins by framing (pre-selecting) Word Cards the individual would be able to use for building their own, unique sentence of three or more words. With practice, the individual will create their own sentence using more Word Cards, until pre-selecting/framing choices are no longer available.

*A three-word sentence example:* **The Dogs Sat.**

The  dogs  sat

*A eight-word sentence example:* **A big brown bear ran to the tree**

A  big  brown  bear  ran

to  the  tree

# Parts of Speech: Classifying Words as Nouns and Pronouns

Assisting a learner to increase their skill to recognize parts of speech is an important ability that improves reading comprehension and writing competency.

In this *Reading With Ease: An Alternative Method, Volume 1* classifying words into the first two of eight parts of speech provides a good foundation for deepening a learner's understanding of sentence structure. Provide scaffolded learner support [i.e., fading support over time] using the word picture cards from volume 1 stories to place the cards into one of two categories: Nouns and Pronouns.

A **Noun** commonly refers to a person or persons, places, or things [examples: girl, boy, dog, home, and meadow].

A **Pronoun** is a word that commonly stands in for an already mentioned noun or as a reference to oneself and other persons [examples: he, she, they, we, I, me, and them].

Each *Reading With Ease: An Alternative Method* volume builds on the process of classifying words as parts of speech.

On the following page, are headings to copy and use to provide clues as to the words that belong to each part of speech. It is also helpful to use the www.dictionary.com app or website to assist a learner in identifying the part of speech a particular word belongs to.

# Nouns

# Pronouns

# Appendix
## Master Word List Data Sheet
### (Track progress over time, copy this page often as needed)

| Word | Story Number | The Date a Word is Mastered | Word | Story Number | The Date a Word is Mastered |
|---|---|---|---|---|---|
| a | 2 | | blue | 18 | |
| about | 5 | | boy | 1 | |
| across | 13 | | bring | 13 | |
| all | 6 | | brother | 7 | |
| am | 20 | | brown | 3 | |
| an | 4 | | buy | 7 | |
| and | 5 | | by | 18 | |
| are | 10 | | called | 15 | |
| as | 15 | | came | 13 | |
| at | 12 | | can (verb) | 4 | |
| ate | 20 | | can (noun) | 13 | |
| away | 19 | | cat | 2 | |
| be | 15 | | chair | 3 | |
| bear | 3 | | charm | 12 | |
| been | 14 | | chicken | 7 | |
| big | 18 | | children | 9 | |
| birthday | 7 | | cloud | 16 | |
| black | 20 | | come | 9 | |

# Master Word List Data Sheet
## (Track progress over time, copy this page often as needed)

| Word | Story Number | The Date a Word is Mastered | | Word | Story Number | The Date a Word is Mastered |
|---|---|---|---|---|---|---|
| computer | 18 | | | fails | 16 | |
| cost | 14 | | | family's | 15 | |
| could | 10 | | | farm | 12 | |
| cow | 11 | | | father | 1 | |
| cut | 15 | | | favorite | 20 | |
| day | 3 | | | find | 17 | |
| did | 12 | | | firewood | 15 | |
| dime | 14 | | | first | 11 | |
| do | 8 | | | floats | 9 | |
| dog | 1 | | | flowers | 10 | |
| dogs | 6 | | | for | 6 | |
| down | 16 | | | friends | 17 | |
| drop | 16 | | | from | 2 | |
| duck | 12 | | | full | 20 | |
| ducks | 12 | | | fun | 6 | |
| each | 16 | | | funny | 19 | |
| elephant | 4 | | | games | 8 | |
| enjoy | 12 | | | gaming | 17 | |

| Word | Story Number | The Date a Word is Mastered | | Word | Story Number | The Date a Word is Mastered |
|---|---|---|---|---|---|---|
| garden | 10 | | | in | 2 | |
| gave | 7 | | | into | 2 | |
| get | 18 | | | is | 1 | |
| girl | 1 | | | if | 3 | |
| go | 17 | | | its | 4 | |
| good | 1 | | | jump | 19 | |
| great | 17 | | | kitten | 7 | |
| green | 14 | | | know | 8 | |
| grew | 15 | | | laugh | 6 | |
| had | 11 | | | lime | 14 | |
| handyman | 15 | | | little | 19 | |
| he | 11 | | | long | 14 | |
| help | 19 | | | look | 12 | |
| here | 19 | | | loudly | 19 | |
| house | 2 | | | love | 9 | |
| how | 10 | | | made | 9 | |
| I | 7 | | | make | 8 | |
| if | 10 | | | makes | 8 | |

# Master Word List Data Sheet
## (Track progress over time, copy this page often as needed)

| Word | Story Number | The Date a Word is Mastered | Word | Story Number | The Date a Word is Mastered |
|---|---|---|---|---|---|
| garden | 10 | | in | 2 | |
| gave | 7 | | into | 2 | |
| get | 18 | | is | 1 | |
| girl | 1 | | if | 3 | |
| go | 17 | | its | 4 | |
| good | 1 | | jump | 19 | |
| great | 17 | | kitten | 7 | |
| green | 14 | | know | 8 | |
| grew | 15 | | laugh | 6 | |
| had | 11 | | lime | 14 | |
| handyman | 15 | | little | 19 | |
| he | 11 | | long | 14 | |
| help | 19 | | look | 12 | |
| here | 19 | | loudly | 19 | |
| house | 2 | | love | 9 | |
| how | 10 | | made | 9 | |
| I | 7 | | make | 8 | |
| if | 10 | | makes | 8 | |

# Master Word List Data Sheet
(Track progress over time, copy this page often as needed)

| Word | Story Number | The Date a Word is Mastered | | Word | Story Number | The Date a Word is Mastered |
|---|---|---|---|---|---|---|
| man | 15 | | | on | 3 | |
| many | 3 | | | one | 3 | |
| me | 7 | | | or | 16 | |
| more | 14 | | | our | 20 | |
| morning | 11 | | | out | 18 | |
| mother | 1 | | | parade | 9 | |
| mouse | 2 | | | part | 18 | |
| must | 20 | | | people | 3 | |
| my | 7 | | | person | 8 | |
| need | 18 | | | planes | 8 | |
| night | 1 | | | play | 6 | |
| no | 18 | | | please | 13 | |
| nose | 4 | | | plowed | 16 | |
| not | 11 | | | ran | 2 | |
| now | 11 | | | rain | 16 | |
| number | 9 | | | rice | 29 | |
| of | 9 | | | run | 19 | |
| oil | 13 | | | said | 13 | |

# Master Word List Data Sheet
## (Track progress over time, copy this page often as needed)

| Word | Story Number | The Date a Word is Mastered | | Word | Story Number | The Date a Word is Mastered |
|---|---|---|---|---|---|---|
| sat | 2 | | | them | 17 | |
| saw | 3 | | | there | 10 | |
| sea | 5 | | | they | 5 | |
| see | 5 | | | this | 10 | |
| since | 14 | | | those | 13 | |
| sit | 5 | | | three | 19 | |
| sleeping | 1 | | | time | 14 | |
| snowflake | 16 | | | to | 9 | |
| so | 2 | | | trains | 8 | |
| some | 8 | | | tree | 5 | |
| squirt | 4 | | | trunk | 4 | |
| store | 17 | | | try | 20 | |
| stories | 5 | | | two | 6 | |
| tell | 19 | | | under | 5 | |
| than | 14 | | | up | 15 | |
| that | 18 | | | use | 11 | |
| the | 1 | | | wanted | 7 | |
| their | 6 | | | was | 11 | |

# Master Word List Data Sheet
(Track progress over time, copy this page often as needed)

| Word | Story Number | The Date a Word is Mastered |
|---|---|---|
| watch | 6 | |
| water | 4 | |
| way | 17 | |
| we | 6 | |
| went | 12 | |
| what | 17 | |
| when | 12 | |
| which | 16 | |
| who | 8 | |
| will | 9 | |
| with | 17 | |
| words | 11 | |
| workers | 13 | |
| would | 10 | |
| write | 5 | |
| yard | 13 | |
| yellow | 10 | |
| you | 4 | |
| your | 4 | |

# Afterword

YES! There are six (6) more volumes in the planning stage that will complete this first series of Reading With Ease: An Alternative Method. Each supplementary volume will include two hundred additional words from Fry's word list.

Each word will be paired with representational images as well as phoneme visual breakdowns. And, similar to this Volume 1, there will be twenty short stories, each comprised of ten unfamiliar words.

May your learner's reading journey be filled with the joy of discovering the wonders of written language!

Kindest regards.

*Elaine M. Peters*

9 781965 007501